I0006452

Table Of Contents

~ Welcome & What You'll Learn

Section I: Introduction to Microsoft Project

Section II: Initial Setup and Navigation

Section III: Building Your Project Plan

Section IV: Resource Management Essentials

Section V: Scheduling and Baselines

Section VI: Tracking Project Progress

Section VII: Working with Views and Tables

Appendices

- **Appendix A:** Glossary of Project Management and MS Project Terms
- **Appendix B:** Quick Reference Guide to Common Shortcuts and Commands
- **Appendix C:** Recommended Resources for Further Learning

Welcome & What You'll Learn

Welcome to *Mastering Microsoft Project: From Setup to Success*! Whether you're a seasoned project manager or just beginning your journey, this book is designed to be your ultimate guide to mastering Microsoft Project and using it effectively to manage projects of any size or complexity.

Microsoft Project is a powerful tool that can transform how you plan, schedule, track, and deliver projects. However, like any sophisticated tool, its true potential unfolds only when you understand how to use it effectively. This book bridges the gap between the software's technical features and the real-world application of project management principles, empowering you to lead your projects to success confidently.

Why This Book?

Microsoft Project is rich in features, but navigating and leveraging them can feel overwhelming without clear guidance. This book simplifies the learning curve by breaking down concepts, features, and techniques into manageable steps. You'll gain not just technical proficiency but also insights into applying these tools to solve common project management challenges.

This guide is tailored for a broad audience, including:

- **Beginners**: New users will find step-by-step instructions for setting up and navigating Microsoft Project.
- **Intermediate Users**: Those with some experience can deepen their understanding of advanced features like resource management, baselines, and cross-project dependencies.
- **Experienced Project Managers**: Even seasoned professionals will discover tips, tricks, and strategies for optimizing workflows and mastering advanced techniques.

What You'll Learn

Throughout this book, you'll embark on a comprehensive journey that equips you with the knowledge and skills to excel in using Microsoft Project. Here's an overview of what you'll gain:

1. Mastering the Basics

- Understand the role of Microsoft Project in project management.
- Learn how to install, configure, and navigate the interface.
- Gain confidence in creating and setting up your first project file.

2. Building Effective Project Plans

- Organize and sequence tasks to reflect your project's scope.
- Define milestones to track critical points in your schedule.
- Use constraints and dependencies to establish realistic timelines.

3. Managing Resources with Precision

- Introduce and assign resources effectively.
- Resolve overallocations and balance workloads.
- Track resource utilization across single and multiple projects.

4. Staying on Schedule and Budget

- Leverage baselines to measure project progress.
- Monitor critical paths to keep your projects on track.

- Adjust task durations and dependencies dynamically.

5. Tracking Progress and Performance

- Update tasks and track percent completion.
- Compare baseline vs. actual performance.
- Use visual indicators to gain actionable insights.

6. Enhancing Collaboration and Reporting

- Share files and integrate with Microsoft 365 tools.
- Generate impactful reports and dashboards for stakeholders.
- Export data to share insights with broader audiences.

7. Exploring Advanced Techniques

- Work with master projects, subprojects, and cross-project dependencies.
- Use custom fields, formulas, and macros for efficiency.
- Embrace hybrid methodologies like Agile while working in Microsoft Project.

8. Closing Projects and Learning for the Future

- Finalize project deliverables and documentation.
- Capture lessons learned and archive templates for reuse.
- Plan your ongoing learning to stay current with updates and best practices.

How to Use This Book

The book is structured into sections that guide you logically from foundational topics to more advanced techniques. You can read it sequentially to build your knowledge step-by-step or jump to specific chapters that address your immediate needs. Each chapter includes practical examples, detailed walkthroughs, and actionable tips to help you apply what you've learned directly to your projects.

Let's Get Started!

With *Mastering Microsoft Project: From Setup to Success*, you're not just learning software; you're building the skills to manage projects with clarity, confidence, and precision. So, let's dive in and begin your journey to project management mastery!

Section I:
Introduction to Microsoft Project

Understanding the Role of Project Management

Project management is at the heart of any successful endeavor, whether you're developing a product, constructing infrastructure, or launching a service. It involves coordinating resources, timelines, and deliverables to achieve objectives effectively and efficiently. Before diving into the specifics of Microsoft Project, it's essential to understand the fundamental principles of project management and its importance in driving organizational success.

What is Project Management?

At its core, project management is the application of processes, methods, skills, and knowledge to achieve specific objectives within defined constraints, such as time, cost, and scope. A project is a temporary endeavor with a start and end date, aimed at creating a unique product, service, or result.

Project management revolves around three key components:

1. **Scope**: Defining what the project will deliver and ensuring it aligns with stakeholder expectations.
2. **Time**: Developing schedules and ensuring timely completion of tasks.
3. **Cost**: Allocating resources within a defined budget to achieve project goals.

Balancing these elements, often referred to as the "triple constraint," is crucial for successful project management.

Why Project Management Matters

Effective project management delivers numerous benefits, including:

- **Clarity of Objectives**: Clearly defined goals ensure all stakeholders are aligned.
- **Efficient Resource Utilization**: Resources, whether people, materials, or finances, are allocated and used optimally.
- **Risk Mitigation**: Potential risks are identified and managed proactively.
- **Stakeholder Satisfaction**: Meeting deadlines, staying within budget, and delivering quality results improve stakeholder trust.
- **Continuous Improvement**: Lessons learned from each project enhance future performance.

Core Principles of Project Management

To excel as a project manager, it's essential to understand and apply these core principles:

1. Initiating Projects

Every project begins with identifying a need or opportunity. During this phase, key objectives are outlined, stakeholders are identified, and a preliminary scope is established. A project charter or brief is often created to formally authorize the project.

2. Planning for Success

Planning is the cornerstone of project management. A detailed project plan defines:

- **Tasks and Activities**: Breaking the project into manageable components.
- **Schedules**: Establishing timelines and milestones.
- **Resources**: Allocating team members, equipment, and budgets.
- **Risks**: Identifying potential challenges and devising mitigation strategies.

3. Executing the Plan

Execution involves putting the plan into action. Teams work on tasks, resources are utilized, and deliverables are produced. Communication and collaboration are critical to ensure the project stays on track.

4. Monitoring and Controlling

Projects rarely go exactly as planned. This phase involves tracking progress, measuring performance against baselines, and making adjustments to address deviations. Tools like Microsoft Project play a vital role in this stage.

5. Closing the Project

At the conclusion, deliverables are finalized, stakeholders sign off, and lessons learned are documented for future projects. This ensures continuous improvement and maximizes the value derived from the project.

The Role of Project Managers

Project managers are the linchpins of successful projects. They coordinate efforts across teams, communicate with stakeholders, and ensure that objectives are met within constraints. Key responsibilities include:

- Defining project scope, goals, and deliverables.
- Planning schedules and allocating resources.
- Monitoring progress and addressing challenges.
- Ensuring quality standards are met.
- Leading and motivating teams.

Microsoft Project empowers project managers by providing a centralized platform to plan, monitor, and manage all aspects of their projects effectively.

How Microsoft Project Supports Project Management

Microsoft Project is a robust tool specifically designed to support the principles of project management. It helps you:

- **Plan and Schedule**: Define tasks, dependencies, and timelines with ease.
- **Allocate Resources**: Assign team members and manage workloads efficiently.
- **Track Progress**: Monitor performance against baselines and adjust plans dynamically.
- **Generate Reports**: Communicate project status and insights with stakeholders effectively.
- **Manage Risks**: Identify potential bottlenecks and make informed decisions to stay on track.

By combining traditional project management principles with the capabilities of Microsoft Project, you can enhance your ability to deliver successful projects, regardless of their size or complexity.

Key Takeaways

1. Project management is essential for delivering objectives on time, within scope, and on budget.
2. Understanding core principles like initiation, planning, execution, monitoring, and closure is crucial for success.

3. Effective project managers balance the triple constraint and drive collaboration, communication, and execution.
4. Microsoft Project is a powerful ally in implementing project management principles, providing tools to plan, track, and report effectively.

In the next chapter, we will explore the different versions and features of Microsoft Project to help you select the best option for your needs.

Exploring Microsoft Project Versions and Features

Microsoft Project is one of the most popular and robust tools for project management, designed to help professionals organize, schedule, and track projects efficiently. With several versions tailored to different needs and feature sets, choosing the right one can significantly enhance your productivity. In this chapter, we'll explore the various editions and features of Microsoft Project, ensuring you have the information needed to select the best version for your requirements.

Overview of Microsoft Project Versions

Microsoft Project is available in several versions, each catering to specific use cases. These versions include both desktop applications and cloud-based solutions, offering flexibility to users depending on their project management needs.

1. Microsoft Project Standard

This is the entry-level version of Microsoft Project, designed for individuals or small teams working on straightforward projects.
Key Features:

- Basic project planning and scheduling.
- Task management with Gantt charts.
- Manual and automatic task scheduling options.
- Limited reporting capabilities.
  Best For: Single users managing small-scale projects with minimal collaboration requirements.

2. Microsoft Project Professional

A more advanced version, Project Professional, adds enhanced collaboration and resource management features.
Key Features:

- Integration with Project Server or Project Online for team collaboration.
- Resource management tools for tracking availability and workloads.
- Advanced reporting and dashboards.
- Compatibility with Microsoft 365 for better collaboration.
  Best For: Project managers working on mid-to-large-scale projects requiring resource allocation and team coordination.

3. Microsoft Project Online

This cloud-based solution provides the flexibility of working on projects anytime, anywhere. Available in multiple plans, it supports team collaboration and project portfolio management.
Key Features:

- Web-based access to project files.
- Collaboration tools integrated with Microsoft Teams and SharePoint.
- Real-time updates and sharing for distributed teams.
- Portfolio and demand management tools.
  Best For: Organizations with distributed teams or those requiring enterprise-level project portfolio management.

4. Microsoft Project for the Web

This lightweight, web-based version is ideal for organizations looking for simplicity and easy integration with other Microsoft 365 tools.
Key Features:

- Drag-and-drop task management with a user-friendly interface.
- Integration with Power BI for advanced reporting.
- Seamless collaboration via Microsoft Teams.
  Best For: Teams that need straightforward project management tools without the complexity of traditional Microsoft Project versions.

5. Microsoft Project Server

Project Server is an enterprise-level solution that provides robust project and portfolio management (PPM) capabilities.
Key Features:

- Centralized project and portfolio management.
- Advanced reporting and business intelligence tools.
- Integration with enterprise resource pools.
  Best For: Large organizations managing multiple projects and portfolios.

Key Features of Microsoft Project

Regardless of the version you choose, Microsoft Project offers a suite of tools designed to streamline project management. Below are some of the most impactful features:

1. Task Management

- Create tasks and subtasks to define the scope of your project.
- Use dependencies (Finish-to-Start, Start-to-Start, etc.) to sequence tasks.
- Assign priorities and durations to each task.

2. Gantt Chart Visualization

- Visualize project timelines and task relationships with Gantt charts.
- Highlight critical paths to identify tasks that directly impact project deadlines.

3. Resource Management

- Assign resources (people, materials, and costs) to tasks.
- Monitor workloads and resolve overallocations.
- Track resource availability and utilization.

4. Scheduling and Baselines

- Use built-in scheduling engines for manual or automatic task planning.
- Set baselines to compare planned vs. actual progress.

5. Reporting and Dashboards

- Generate predefined and custom reports to track performance.
- Use visual dashboards for at-a-glance updates on project health, resource allocation, and timelines.

6. Integration with Microsoft Ecosystem

- Collaborate through Microsoft Teams, SharePoint, and OneDrive.

- Export data to Excel or Power BI for further analysis.

7. Portfolio Management

- Evaluate and prioritize multiple projects within a portfolio.
- Allocate resources across projects for optimal efficiency.
- Analyze risks and opportunities at the portfolio level.

8. Customizable Fields and Views

- Add custom fields to track unique project metrics.
- Create tailored views to focus on specific aspects of your project.

Choosing the Right Version for Your Needs

To decide which version of Microsoft Project best suits your needs, consider the following:

1. **Project Complexity**: Smaller projects may only require Microsoft Project Standard, while larger, more complex projects may benefit from Professional or Online versions.
2. **Team Size**: Cloud-based solutions like Project Online or Project for the Web are ideal for distributed teams.
3. **Budget**: While Standard offers basic functionality at a lower cost, enterprise solutions like Project Server require more significant investment.
4. **Collaboration Needs**: For teams requiring seamless communication and real-time updates, Project Online or integrations with Microsoft Teams are crucial.

Microsoft Project: Empowering Effective Management

Microsoft Project's diverse range of versions and features ensures that it meets the needs of all types of project managers, from individuals working on small-scale tasks to enterprises managing portfolios. Understanding the tools available at your disposal is the first step in mastering this powerful software.

In the next chapter, we'll guide you through the installation and configuration process, ensuring you're set up and ready to begin leveraging Microsoft Project effectively.

Installing and Configuring Microsoft Project

Proper installation and configuration of Microsoft Project are essential to begin your journey in project management. This chapter provides a step-by-step guide to acquiring, installing, and configuring Microsoft Project to ensure you're ready to build, manage, and track projects effectively.

1. Acquiring Microsoft Project

Before installation, it's important to choose the right version of Microsoft Project based on your project management needs.

Subscription and Licensing Options

Microsoft Project is available as:

- **Subscription Plans (Microsoft 365)**: Project Plan 1, Plan 3, and Plan 5 offer varying levels of features, from lightweight task management to enterprise portfolio management.
- **Perpetual Licenses**: Standard and Professional editions are available as one-time purchases, ideal for offline use.

Where to Purchase

You can purchase Microsoft Project from:

- Microsoft's official website (Office.com).
- Authorized Microsoft resellers or retailers.
- Your organization's licensing agreement, if applicable.

System Requirements

Ensure your computer meets the minimum system requirements:

- **Operating System**: Windows 10 or later (for desktop versions).
- **Processor**: 1.6 GHz or faster, dual-core recommended.
- **Memory**: At least 4 GB RAM; 8 GB or more recommended for larger projects.
- **Storage**: 4 GB of available hard disk space.
- **Display**: 1280 x 768 screen resolution or higher.
- **Internet**: Required for online versions and cloud-based features.

2. Installing Microsoft Project

Step-by-Step Installation Process for Desktop Versions

1. **Download Microsoft Project**
   - Log in to your Microsoft account.
   - Navigate to the "My Account" page or use the provided product key.
   - Download the setup file for Microsoft Project.
2. **Run the Installer**
   - Open the downloaded file and follow the on-screen instructions.
   - Choose the installation type:
     - **Default Install**: Installs all components in a predefined location.
     - **Custom Install**: Allows you to select specific components and installation paths.

3. **Activate Microsoft Project**
   - Enter your product key or log in with your Microsoft 365 credentials.
   - Verify the activation status in the application settings.

Accessing Microsoft Project Online

1. Log in to your Microsoft 365 account.
2. Navigate to the Microsoft Project Online portal.
3. Launch the application directly from your browser without downloading any software.

---

3. Configuring Microsoft Project

Once installed, configuring Microsoft Project is critical for a smooth and personalized experience.

Setting Up Initial Preferences

1. **Open Microsoft Project**
   Launch the application to access the default workspace.
2. **Configure Default Options**
   Navigate to: **File > Options**.
   - **General**: Set your default project view, theme, and username.
   - **Schedule**: Adjust settings such as default task mode (manual or automatic) and working hours.
   - **Proofing**: Customize spell check and grammar preferences.
   - **Save**: Specify default save locations, including cloud storage like OneDrive or SharePoint.
3. **Enable Add-Ins**
   - Go to **File > Options > Add-Ins**.
   - Enable or disable third-party tools to enhance functionality, such as Power BI for reporting.

---

4. Customizing the Working Environment

Setting Up Working Calendars

One of the first tasks in any project is configuring a calendar to match the working schedule of your organization.

- Navigate to: **Project > Change Working Time**.
- Define working days, hours, and holidays.
- Save the calendar as the default for all new projects if necessary.

Customizing the Ribbon and Quick Access Toolbar

Streamline your workflow by personalizing the user interface:

1. Go to **File > Options > Customize Ribbon**.
2. Add or remove tabs and commands based on your frequent tasks.
3. Adjust the Quick Access Toolbar to include shortcuts for commonly used features like "Save," "Undo," and "Baseline."

---

5. Verifying Configuration for Team Collaboration

If you're working in a collaborative environment, ensure your setup supports team workflows:

- **Cloud Storage**: Link your OneDrive or SharePoint account to save and share files effortlessly.
- **Permissions**: For Project Online users, assign appropriate permissions to team members.
- **Integration**: Verify integration with tools like Microsoft Teams for real-time communication.

---

6. Troubleshooting Installation and Configuration Issues

Common Installation Issues

1. **Activation Errors**:
   - Ensure the product key is valid and not used on multiple devices.
   - Verify your Microsoft 365 subscription status.
2. **System Compatibility**:
   - Double-check that your system meets the minimum requirements.
   - Update your operating system or drivers if necessary.

Configuration Challenges

1. **Add-Ins Not Functioning**:
   - Ensure add-ins are compatible with your version of Microsoft Project.
   - Enable or reinstall the add-ins via the "Options" menu.
2. **Calendar Settings Not Applied**:
   - Confirm that the calendar is set as the default for the project.
   - Recheck the working hours and holidays defined in the calendar.

---

7. Getting Started with Your First Project

With Microsoft Project installed and configured, you're ready to create your first project. In the next section, we'll explore how to navigate the user interface and set up a new project file to begin managing tasks, resources, and schedules efficiently.

Key Takeaways

- Microsoft Project offers desktop and online versions to suit varying needs.
- Proper installation ensures that all tools and features are readily available.
- Configuring default settings, calendars, and user preferences saves time and enhances efficiency.
- Addressing installation and configuration issues promptly ensures a smooth start.

By following these steps, you've laid a strong foundation for leveraging Microsoft Project to its full potential.

Section II:
Initial Setup and Navigation

Navigating the Ribbon and Interface

Microsoft Project's user interface is designed to provide easy access to powerful tools and features while maintaining a logical and organized structure. Mastering the navigation of the ribbon and interface is a crucial first step in using Microsoft Project effectively. This chapter will guide you through the key elements of the interface, ensuring you're familiar with its layout and functionalities.

1. Understanding the Microsoft Project Interface

When you open Microsoft Project, you are greeted by a workspace that is organized into several distinct areas. Here's an overview of the main components:

1.1 The Ribbon

The ribbon is the central command center in Microsoft Project, offering tabs that group tools and features into logical categories. The ribbon is context-sensitive, meaning it displays relevant options depending on what you are working on.

Key Ribbon Tabs

- **File**: Access options for saving, opening, exporting, and printing files.
- **Task**: Manage tasks, create new ones, assign resources, and adjust schedules.
- **Resource**: Add and assign resources, resolve overallocations, and manage resource usage.
- **Report**: Generate predefined and custom reports, and view project insights.
- **Project**: Set baselines, define working calendars, and adjust project settings.
- **View**: Customize how information is displayed, switch views, and modify tables.

1.2 Quick Access Toolbar

Located above the ribbon, this toolbar provides shortcuts to frequently used commands like Save, Undo, and Redo. You can customize the Quick Access Toolbar to include commands you use regularly.

1.3 The Workspace Area

This is the central area where project data is displayed. It includes:

- **Gantt Chart View**: Displays tasks, timelines, and dependencies.
- **Task Table**: A grid for entering and editing task details like name, duration, and start/end dates.
- **Timeline View**: Offers a high-level view of your project schedule.

1.4 The Status Bar

At the bottom of the interface, the status bar displays project-related information, such as the current view, zoom level, and task filter status.

2. Navigating the Ribbon

The ribbon is divided into tabs, each containing related commands grouped logically. Let's explore the most commonly used tabs:

2.1 Task Tab

The Task tab focuses on managing tasks in your project.

- **Add Task**: Quickly insert new tasks into your project plan.
- **Link Tasks**: Create dependencies between tasks.
- **Task Mode**: Switch between manual and automatic scheduling modes.
- **Task Inspector**: Analyze and resolve scheduling conflicts.

2.2 Resource Tab

The Resource tab is essential for managing team members, materials, and costs.

- **Add Resources**: Enter resource details into the project.
- **Assign Resources**: Link resources to specific tasks.
- **Leveling Options**: Resolve resource overallocations automatically.

2.3 Report Tab

The Report tab offers tools for visualizing project data.

- **Dashboards**: Generate visual summaries of project status.
- **Custom Reports**: Build tailored reports to meet specific stakeholder needs.
- **Visual Reports**: Export data to Excel or Visio for advanced analysis.

2.4 View Tab

The View tab lets you customize how project information is presented.

- **Task Views**: Switch between Gantt Chart, Calendar, and Network Diagram views.
- **Resource Views**: Focus on resource assignments and workloads.
- **Filters**: Apply filters to focus on specific tasks or resources.

---

3. Customizing the Interface

3.1 Personalizing the Ribbon

You can modify the ribbon to suit your workflow:

- Navigate to **File > Options > Customize Ribbon**.
- Add or remove tabs and groups as needed.
- Save your customizations for future projects.

3.2 Adjusting the Quick Access Toolbar

- Right-click any command in the ribbon and select **Add to Quick Access Toolbar**.
- Rearrange or remove commands by right-clicking on the toolbar.

3.3 Modifying the Workspace

- Use the **Split View** option to display multiple views simultaneously (e.g., Gantt Chart and Task Details).

- Adjust column widths in the Task Table to prioritize the most relevant data.

---

4. Navigating Views and Tables

Microsoft Project offers several built-in views to accommodate different project management needs.

4.1 Gantt Chart View

This is the default view in Microsoft Project and the most widely used. It displays:

- A table on the left for task details.
- A timeline on the right with bars representing task durations.

4.2 Calendar View

The Calendar view presents tasks on a monthly calendar, making it easy to visualize schedules and deadlines.

4.3 Network Diagram View

This view provides a flowchart-style representation of tasks and their dependencies. It's useful for analyzing project workflows.

4.4 Resource Usage View

Displays resource assignments and workloads, helping you manage resource allocation effectively.

4.5 Task Usage View

Focuses on task assignments and allows you to view work distributed over time.

---

5. Tips for Efficient Navigation

- **Use Keyboard Shortcuts**: Familiarize yourself with common shortcuts (e.g., Ctrl + G to go to a specific task).
- **Search Bar**: Use the built-in search bar at the top of the ribbon to quickly locate commands or features.
- **Right-Click Menus**: Access context-sensitive options by right-clicking on tasks, resources, or other elements.
- **Zoom Controls**: Adjust the timeline scale using the zoom slider in the status bar for better visibility.

---

6. Troubleshooting Interface Challenges

Problem: Missing Ribbon Tabs

- **Solution**: Enable missing tabs through **File > Options > Customize Ribbon**.

Problem: Overcrowded Workspace

- **Solution**: Hide unnecessary columns in the Task Table or collapse ribbon groups to create more space.

Problem: Difficulty Finding Commands

- **Solution**: Use the search bar or customize the ribbon to group frequently used commands.

Key Takeaways

1. The ribbon and interface of Microsoft Project are designed for easy access to essential tools and features.
2. Familiarity with key tabs, such as Task, Resource, and View, enhances navigation efficiency.
3. Customizing the ribbon, Quick Access Toolbar, and workspace can significantly improve productivity.
4. Utilizing views and tables allows you to analyze and present project data in various formats.

By mastering the ribbon and interface, you'll be well-equipped to set up your first project file and begin managing tasks effectively.

Setting Up a New Project File

Creating a new project file is one of the foundational steps in using Microsoft Project effectively. A well-set-up project file serves as the backbone of your project management activities, ensuring all subsequent tasks, resources, and schedules align with your project goals. This chapter will guide you through the process of setting up a new project file, ensuring accuracy and efficiency from the start.

1. Starting a New Project File

Step 1: Launching Microsoft Project

1. Open Microsoft Project on your computer.
2. You will see the **Start Screen** with options to create or open files.

Step 2: Choosing the Blank Project Option

1. Click on **Blank Project** to start with an empty file.
2. Alternatively, you can choose from templates if your project has similar characteristics to a predefined structure.

2. Configuring Basic Project Information

After opening a new file, you need to define the basic details of your project.

Step 1: Set the Project Start Date

1. Navigate to **Project > Project Information**.
2. Enter the **Start Date** or, if applicable, the **Finish Date** (Microsoft Project will calculate the other based on task dependencies and durations).
3. Click **OK** to confirm.

Step 2: Name and Save Your Project

1. Go to **File > Save As** to save the project.
2. Choose a meaningful file name and select the desired location (e.g., local drive, OneDrive, or SharePoint).
3. Set the file format to **.mpp** (Microsoft Project's native file format).

3. Setting Project Calendars

Calendars in Microsoft Project define the working days and hours for your project.

Step 1: Access Calendar Settings

1. Go to **Project > Change Working Time**.

Step 2: Choose or Create a Calendar

- Select one of the default calendars:
  - **Standard**: Standard 8-hour workdays, Monday to Friday.
  - **24 Hours**: Continuous work, 24/7.

-    o **Night Shift**: Specialized for evening and night schedules.
- Customize the calendar if your project has unique working hours or holidays.

Step 3: Set the Default Calendar for the Project

1. Assign the chosen calendar in **Project > Project Information > Calendar**.

---

4. Defining Key Project Settings

Customizing default settings ensures the project aligns with organizational or team-specific standards.

Step 1: Adjust Scheduling Options

1. Go to **File > Options > Schedule**.
2. Set the following:
   - o **New Tasks Created**: Choose between manual or automatic scheduling.
   - o **Default Start and End Times**: Specify typical working hours for tasks.
   - o **Work Week**: Define the work week (e.g., Monday to Friday).

Step 2: Customize Currency and Units

1. Go to **File > Options > Display**.
2. Adjust currency format (e.g., $, €, ¥) to match your project's financial context.
3. Specify default units for resource allocation (e.g., hours, days).

---

5. Entering Initial Project Tasks

While this chapter focuses on setting up the file, entering initial tasks helps define the scope and structure of your project.

Step 1: Add Tasks to the Task Table

1. In the **Gantt Chart View**, enter task names in the **Task Name** column.
2. Use **Tab** or **Enter** to move between rows and columns.

Step 2: Define Task Durations

1. In the **Duration** column, specify how long each task will take (e.g., 3 days, 5 hours).
2. Leave the duration as **TBD** if it's not yet determined.

Step 3: Sequence Tasks (Optional)

You can link tasks at this stage to define dependencies:

1. Highlight two tasks.
2. Click **Task > Link Tasks** to create a Finish-to-Start relationship.

---

6. Setting Baselines (Optional at This Stage)

While baselines are typically set after planning, you can define an initial baseline as a placeholder:

1. Go to **Project > Set Baseline > Set Baseline**.
2. Choose **Baseline 1** (or any other unused baseline).

3. Click **OK** to save it.

---

7. Saving and Sharing Your Project File

Step 1: Save Your Work Regularly

1. Use **Ctrl + S** or go to **File > Save** to prevent data loss.

Step 2: Save to the Cloud (Optional)

1. Link your Microsoft 365 account to save directly to OneDrive or SharePoint for easy access and collaboration.

Step 3: Share with Team Members

1. Go to **File > Share** to send the project file via email or invite team members to collaborate using cloud storage.

---

8. Best Practices for Setting Up a New Project File

1. **Start with Accurate Dates**: Ensure the start date reflects reality to avoid rescheduling issues later.
2. **Use Descriptive Task Names**: Clarity in task naming helps everyone understand the scope of each task.
3. **Save Early and Often**: Regularly save your file to avoid data loss.
4. **Customize Calendars**: Use a calendar that aligns with your team's working hours and holidays.
5. **Double-Check Settings**: Verify that default settings align with your project's needs before proceeding.

Common Issues and Troubleshooting

Problem: Tasks are not scheduling correctly.

- **Solution**: Check the project calendar and task dependencies for inconsistencies.

Problem: The start date of the project doesn't match your expectation.

- **Solution**: Adjust the project start date in **Project > Project Information**.

Problem: Unable to share the file with team members.

- **Solution**: Ensure the file is saved in a shared location (e.g., OneDrive or SharePoint) and permissions are set correctly.

Key Takeaways

1. Setting up a new project file is the foundation of effective project management in Microsoft Project.
2. Defining project details, calendars, and settings ensures consistency and accuracy.
3. Saving and sharing the project file facilitates collaboration and prevents data loss.

With your project file set up, you're ready to dive deeper into defining calendars and working times, which we'll cover in the next chapter. This will help you customize the schedule and accommodate unique working hours for your team or organization.

Defining Project Calendars and Working Time

Calendars are a fundamental component of project planning in Microsoft Project. They define the working days, hours, and non-working time for your project. By accurately configuring calendars, you ensure that schedules reflect realistic timelines, accommodate team availability, and account for holidays or specific work shifts. In this chapter, we'll guide you through the process of defining project calendars and setting working time in Microsoft Project.

1. Understanding Project Calendars

1.1 Types of Calendars in Microsoft Project

Microsoft Project uses three types of calendars:

- **Base Calendars**: Define general working and non-working times. These can be applied to the entire project, specific tasks, or individual resources.
- **Project Calendar**: A default calendar that dictates the working time for the entire project.
- **Resource Calendars**: Define the availability of specific resources (e.g., team members, equipment).

1.2 Importance of Configuring Calendars

- Reflects organizational working hours and holidays.
- Ensures accurate scheduling of tasks.
- Prevents resource overallocation by aligning task schedules with resource availability.

2. Setting the Project Calendar

The project calendar serves as the default schedule for all tasks unless overridden by a resource or task calendar.

Step 1: Access the Project Calendar

1. Navigate to **Project > Change Working Time**.
2. The dialog box will display the current calendar.

Step 2: Select or Create a Calendar

- **Choose a Default Calendar**:
    - **Standard**: 8-hour workdays, Monday to Friday (default).
    - **24 Hours**: Continuous work schedule (e.g., factories or hospitals).
    - **Night Shift**: Evening and night shifts.
- **Create a Custom Calendar**:
    - Click **Create New Calendar**.
    - Name your calendar and select **Make a Copy of [Base Calendar]**.
    - Modify working times as needed.

Step 3: Set the Project Calendar

1. Go to **Project > Project Information**.
2. Select your desired calendar from the **Calendar** dropdown.
3. Click **OK** to apply the calendar to the project.

3. Customizing Working Time

Step 1: Adjust Default Working Hours

1. In the **Change Working Time** dialog box, select the desired calendar.
2. Click the **Work Weeks** tab and then **Details**.
3. Specify default working hours for each day (e.g., 9:00 AM–5:00 PM with a lunch break).

Step 2: Add Non-Working Time (Holidays)

1. In the **Exceptions** tab, add non-working days (e.g., public holidays, company events).
2. Enter the exception name, start date, and end date.
3. Save the calendar to apply changes.

4. Applying Custom Calendars to Tasks and Resources

Sometimes, specific tasks or resources require unique calendars.

4.1 Assigning a Calendar to a Task

1. Select the task in the **Task Table**.
2. Navigate to **Task > Information**.
3. In the **Advanced** tab, assign a specific calendar using the **Calendar** dropdown.
4. Check **Scheduling Ignores Resource Calendars** if the task schedule should override resource availability.

4.2 Assigning a Calendar to a Resource

1. Go to **View > Resource Sheet**.
2. Select the resource and open the **Resource Information** dialog box.
3. Assign the appropriate calendar under the **General** tab.

5. Using Multiple Calendars

Microsoft Project allows you to use multiple calendars to manage complex projects.

5.1 Task-Specific Calendars

For tasks that require work during off-hours or weekends, create a custom calendar and assign it to those tasks.

5.2 Resource-Specific Calendars

Use resource calendars to account for individual work schedules, such as part-time employees or contractors working different hours.

5.3 Combining Calendars

When multiple calendars are in use, Microsoft Project resolves scheduling conflicts by combining them:

- Task calendars take precedence over resource calendars unless otherwise specified.

6. Tips for Efficient Calendar Management

1. **Standardize Calendars**: Use a consistent set of calendars across similar projects to maintain uniformity.
2. **Account for Non-Working Time Early**: Enter holidays and planned downtimes during the initial setup to avoid rescheduling later.
3. **Verify Calendar Assignments**: Regularly check task and resource calendars to ensure accuracy.
4. **Document Customizations**: Keep a record of changes made to calendars for reference and consistency in future projects.

---

7. Troubleshooting Calendar Issues

Problem: Tasks not scheduled as expected.

- **Solution**: Check if a task-specific calendar or resource calendar is overriding the project calendar.

Problem: Non-working time not reflected in the schedule.

- **Solution**: Verify that holidays or exceptions have been added correctly to the assigned calendar.

Problem: Resource overallocation warnings.

- **Solution**: Ensure resource calendars match their actual availability.

---

8. Summary

Defining project calendars and working time is critical for creating accurate schedules and managing resource availability. By customizing calendars to align with your project's unique needs, you set the stage for effective planning and execution.

Key Takeaways

- Calendars define working and non-working times for projects, tasks, and resources.
- The project calendar serves as the default schedule, but custom calendars can be applied for specific needs.
- Accurate calendar setup ensures realistic schedules and prevents resource conflicts.

In the next chapter, we'll explore how to customize default settings in Microsoft Project, allowing you to further streamline your project setup and management processes.

Customizing Default Settings

Customizing default settings in Microsoft Project is a critical step to tailor the software to your organization's standards and your specific project management needs. By configuring these settings, you can save time, enhance efficiency, and ensure consistency across projects. This chapter guides you through the key default settings to adjust and how to customize them effectively.

1. Why Customize Default Settings?

1.1 Improved Efficiency

- Reduces repetitive configuration tasks for each new project.
- Streamlines workflows by pre-setting preferences that align with your processes.

1.2 Enhanced Consistency

- Ensures all team members use the same settings and standards.
- Maintains uniformity across projects, reducing the risk of errors.

1.3 Personalization

- Adapts Microsoft Project to fit your unique project management style and organizational needs.

2. Accessing Default Settings

To customize default settings:

1. Go to **File > Options**.
2. The **Project Options** dialog box appears, presenting several tabs for various settings categories.

3. Key Default Settings to Customize

3.1 General Settings

These settings affect the overall behavior and appearance of Microsoft Project.

1. **Default View**: Set the view that appears when opening a project (e.g., Gantt Chart, Task Sheet).
2. **User Name and Initials**: Specify your name and initials for tracking changes.
   - Navigate to **File > Options > General**.

3.2 Scheduling Options

The Scheduling tab is one of the most critical for project planning.

1. **New Tasks Created**: Choose between manual or automatic scheduling.
   - Manual scheduling allows you to define start and finish dates manually.
   - Automatic scheduling calculates dates based on task dependencies and durations.
2. **Default Task Duration**: Set a standard duration for new tasks (e.g., 1 day, 1 week).
3. **Default Start and End Times**: Configure typical working hours (e.g., 9:00 AM to 5:00 PM).
4. **Week Start Day**: Adjust the calendar to align with your organization's workweek (e.g., Monday or Sunday).

3.3 Proofing and Spelling

Ensure accuracy by customizing proofing options:

1. Enable or disable spell-check features.
2. Add industry-specific terms to the custom dictionary.
    - Navigate to **File > Options > Proofing**.

3.4 Save Options

Control where and how your projects are saved.

1. **Default Save Location**: Set a specific folder or cloud storage (e.g., OneDrive or SharePoint).
2. **File Format**: Choose a default format for saving files (e.g., .mpp, .xml).
    - Navigate to **File > Options > Save**.

3.5 Display Settings

These settings control how information is displayed within Microsoft Project.

1. **Currency**: Adjust the currency symbol and format (e.g., $, €, ¥).
2. **Date Format**: Choose the format for displaying dates (e.g., 1/9/2025 or January 9, 2025).
3. **Gantt Chart Layout**: Customize how bars and labels appear on the Gantt Chart.
    - Navigate to **File > Options > Display**.

3.6 Advanced Settings

For more granular control, customize advanced options:

1. **Calculation Mode**: Decide whether calculations are done automatically or manually.
2. **Baseline Settings**: Set default baselines for measuring project progress.
3. **Time Units**: Choose default time units for tasks (e.g., hours, days, weeks).
    - Navigate to **File > Options > Advanced**.

4. Customizing Default Templates

If you frequently create similar projects, customizing a default project template can save time.

Step 1: Create a New Project Template

1. Open a new project file.
2. Configure settings such as calendars, views, and task structures.
3. Save the file as a template: **File > Save As > Project Template (.mpt)**.

Step 2: Apply the Template

1. When starting a new project, select **New from Template**.
2. Choose your customized template to apply pre-configured settings.

5. Best Practices for Customizing Default Settings

1. **Document Your Standards**: Create a reference guide for team members to ensure consistent use of settings.
2. **Test Configurations**: Before finalizing settings, test them on a sample project to ensure they work as intended.
3. **Incorporate Feedback**: Gather input from team members to identify settings that improve their workflows.
4. **Backup Settings**: Save templates and settings configurations in a secure location for future use.

6. Common Issues and Troubleshooting

Problem: Settings are not applied to new projects.

- **Solution**: Ensure changes are saved to the global template or default project template.

Problem: Incorrect time or date formats appear.

- **Solution**: Adjust regional settings in both Microsoft Project and your operating system.

Problem: Team members using different settings.

- **Solution**: Share templates and standardize settings across the organization.

7. Key Takeaways

1. Customizing default settings saves time, enhances efficiency, and ensures consistency across projects.
2. Key settings include scheduling options, calendars, save preferences, and display formats.
3. Templates provide a powerful way to streamline project creation with pre-configured settings.
4. Regularly review and update settings to reflect evolving project management needs.

By personalizing Microsoft Project's default settings, you create a strong foundation for efficient project management. With these configurations in place, you're ready to start building your project plan, which we'll cover in the next section.

Section III:
Building Your Project Plan

Creating and Organizing Tasks

Tasks are the building blocks of any project plan. In Microsoft Project, tasks represent individual units of work that must be completed to achieve your project's goals. Properly creating and organizing tasks ensures clarity, improves scheduling accuracy, and facilitates tracking progress. This chapter will guide you through the steps to create, structure, and manage tasks effectively in Microsoft Project.

1. Understanding Tasks in Microsoft Project

1.1 Types of Tasks

Microsoft Project supports several types of tasks:

1. **Regular Tasks**: Standard tasks with a specific duration and effort.
2. **Summary Tasks**: Parent tasks that group subtasks, providing an overview of progress and scheduling.
3. **Milestones**: Significant events or deliverables in a project, typically with zero duration.
4. **Recurring Tasks**: Tasks that repeat at regular intervals, such as weekly meetings.

1.2 Importance of Organizing Tasks

- Provides a clear structure and hierarchy for the project.
- Ensures dependencies are accurately established for scheduling.
- Simplifies tracking and reporting by grouping related activities.

2. Creating Tasks

Step 1: Adding Tasks

1. Open your project file in the **Gantt Chart View**.
2. Enter task names directly into the **Task Name** column in the grid.
3. Press **Enter** or **Tab** to move to the next row.

Step 2: Defining Task Durations

1. In the **Duration** column, specify how long the task will take (e.g., 3 days, 5 hours).
2. Use "TBD" for tasks with undefined durations, and update them later.

Step 3: Assigning Start and Finish Dates

1. By default, Microsoft Project calculates start and finish dates based on the project calendar and task dependencies.
2. If needed, manually set specific dates by entering them in the **Start** and **Finish** columns.

3. Organizing Tasks

3.1 Creating a Task Hierarchy

Use indentation to organize tasks into a structured hierarchy:

1. Select the task you want to make a subtask.
2. Click **Task > Indent Task** to nest it under a summary task.
3. To reverse the process, click **Task > Outdent Task**.

3.2 Grouping Tasks into Phases

Group related tasks under summary tasks to represent project phases or workstreams:

1. Enter a summary task name in the **Task Name** column.
2. Add subtasks beneath it and indent them.
3. The summary task will automatically display the total duration and progress of its subtasks.

---

4. Using Milestones

4.1 Adding Milestones

Milestones represent key deliverables or checkpoints in your project:

1. Add a new task and name it.
2. Set its duration to **0 days** to mark it as a milestone.
3. Milestones will appear as diamonds on the Gantt Chart.

4.2 Benefits of Milestones

- Highlights critical project achievements.
- Serves as progress checkpoints for stakeholders.
- Helps monitor adherence to the project schedule.

---

5. Creating Recurring Tasks

Recurring tasks save time when managing activities that occur at regular intervals.

Step 1: Add a Recurring Task

1. Go to **Task > Task > Recurring Task**.
2. Enter the task name and frequency (e.g., daily, weekly, monthly).
3. Specify the start and end dates.
4. Click **OK**, and the recurring tasks will be added to the task list.

Step 2: Managing Recurring Tasks

- Each instance of the recurring task can be updated individually if needed.
- Recurring tasks are grouped under a summary task by default.

---

6. Tips for Efficient Task Management

1. **Use Descriptive Task Names**: Ensure task names clearly define the work to be performed.

2. **Avoid Overlapping Durations**: Ensure durations align with realistic work expectations.
3. **Limit the Use of Manual Dates**: Allow Microsoft Project to calculate dates based on dependencies for more flexibility.
4. **Regularly Review Task Hierarchy**: Keep the task structure logical and consistent.
5. **Leverage Milestones and Recurring Tasks**: Use these features to mark key points and repetitive activities.

---

7. Troubleshooting Task Issues

Problem: Tasks are not appearing in the correct order.

- **Solution**: Review task IDs and re-sort tasks if necessary.

Problem: Duration changes unexpectedly.

- **Solution**: Check for dependencies or constraints affecting the task schedule.

Problem: Recurring tasks are not updating correctly.

- **Solution**: Ensure changes are applied to all instances of the recurring task.

---

8. Summary

Creating and organizing tasks is a critical step in building your project plan. By structuring tasks into a logical hierarchy, defining milestones, and utilizing recurring tasks, you set the stage for effective scheduling, resource management, and progress tracking.

Key Takeaways

- Tasks represent the core elements of your project plan, and their proper creation ensures accurate scheduling.
- Use summary tasks and subtasks to organize work into manageable phases.
- Milestones and recurring tasks add clarity and efficiency to the task list.

In the next chapter, we'll explore linking and sequencing tasks to establish dependencies and create a dynamic, interconnected project schedule.

Linking and Sequencing Tasks

Linking and sequencing tasks in Microsoft Project is crucial for creating a dynamic and logical project schedule. Task dependencies define how tasks relate to one another, and sequencing ensures tasks are performed in the correct order. By mastering these techniques, you can develop an efficient and flexible project plan that adapts to changes.

1. Understanding Task Dependencies

Task dependencies establish the relationships between tasks and dictate how one task affects another. Dependencies are essential for:

- Creating realistic schedules.
- Identifying critical paths and bottlenecks.
- Managing task sequences effectively.

1.1 Types of Task Dependencies

Microsoft Project supports four types of dependencies:

1. **Finish-to-Start (FS)**: The most common dependency where one task must finish before another starts (e.g., "Complete foundation" → "Start building walls").
2. **Start-to-Start (SS)**: Both tasks start at the same time (e.g., "Design blueprint" → "Approve blueprint").
3. **Finish-to-Finish (FF)**: Both tasks finish at the same time (e.g., "Write report" → "Proofread report").
4. **Start-to-Finish (SF)**: Rarely used, where one task starts before another finishes (e.g., "Start new shift" → "End current shift").

2. Linking Tasks

Step 1: Select Tasks to Link

1. Highlight the tasks you want to link by clicking and dragging over their rows in the **Task Name** column.
2. Ensure the tasks are in the correct sequence.

Step 2: Create Links

1. Navigate to **Task > Schedule > Link Tasks** or use the shortcut **Ctrl + F2**.
2. Microsoft Project will automatically create **Finish-to-Start** links between the selected tasks.

Step 3: Adjust Dependencies

1. Double-click the task to open the **Task Information** dialog box.
2. Go to the **Predecessors** tab.
3. Change the **Type** to the desired dependency (e.g., Start-to-Start, Finish-to-Finish).

3. Sequencing Tasks

3.1 Understanding Task IDs

Tasks are sequenced based on their row numbers, which are referred to as Task IDs. Sequencing ensures tasks are arranged logically to reflect the workflow.

3.2 Using the Gantt Chart for Sequencing

1. Drag tasks up or down in the **Task Name** column to reorder them.
2. Ensure dependencies remain intact by checking the **Predecessors** and **Successors** columns.

---

4. Adding Lead and Lag Times

Lead and lag times allow you to fine-tune task schedules.

4.1 Lead Time

Lead time overlaps tasks, enabling the successor task to start before the predecessor finishes.

- Example: Allowing "Start marketing campaign" to begin 2 days before "Develop marketing materials" finishes.

4.2 Lag Time

Lag time creates a delay between the predecessor's finish and the successor's start.

- Example: Adding a 3-day gap between "Paint walls" and "Install fixtures" to allow drying time.

How to Add Lead or Lag Time

1. Open the **Task Information** dialog box.
2. Go to the **Predecessors** tab.
3. Enter the lead or lag time in the **Lag** column (e.g., -2d for 2 days lead, 3d for 3 days lag).

---

5. Using Constraints in Sequencing

Constraints dictate when tasks can start or finish, adding flexibility or rigidity to the schedule.

5.1 Types of Constraints

1. **As Soon As Possible (ASAP)**: Default for most tasks; tasks begin as soon as predecessors are complete.
2. **As Late As Possible (ALAP)**: Tasks are delayed as much as possible without affecting the project deadline.
3. **Must Start On (MSO) / Must Finish On (MFO)**: Specifies exact start or finish dates.
4. **Start No Earlier Than (SNET) / Finish No Earlier Than (FNET)**: Tasks cannot start or finish before a set date.
5. **Start No Later Than (SNLT) / Finish No Later Than (FNLT)**: Tasks must start or finish by a set date.

How to Apply Constraints

1. Select the task and navigate to **Task > Information**.
2. Go to the **Advanced** tab.
3. Select a constraint type and specify a date, if applicable.

---

6. Visualizing Task Dependencies

Microsoft Project provides several tools to visualize and manage dependencies:

6.1 Gantt Chart

- Linked tasks appear as arrows connecting task bars on the Gantt Chart.
- Right-click the chart and select **Layout** to customize dependency line styles.

6.2 Task Path

- Use the **Task Path** feature to highlight specific dependency paths:
  - Go to **Format > Task Path**, and select options like **Predecessors** or **Successors**.

---

7. Tips for Efficient Task Linking and Sequencing

1. **Start with Major Tasks**: Outline major phases or deliverables before breaking them into smaller tasks.
2. **Avoid Excessive Constraints**: Overusing constraints can reduce schedule flexibility.
3. **Review Dependencies Regularly**: Ensure task links accurately reflect the intended workflow.
4. **Document Dependencies**: Maintain a record of critical dependencies for stakeholder reference.
5. **Use Milestones**: Link milestones to major task groups for better tracking of progress.

---

8. Troubleshooting Common Issues

Problem: Tasks are not scheduling as expected.

- **Solution**: Check for incorrect dependencies or conflicting constraints.

Problem: Gantt Chart appears cluttered with dependency lines.

- **Solution**: Filter tasks to show only critical paths or key dependencies.

Problem: Overlapping tasks causing resource conflicts.

- **Solution**: Adjust lead and lag times or modify dependencies to resolve conflicts.

---

9. Summary

Linking and sequencing tasks ensures your project schedule is logical, accurate, and adaptable to changes. By defining dependencies, adjusting lead and lag times, and using constraints strategically, you create a robust project plan that reflects real-world conditions.

Key Takeaways

- Task dependencies (Finish-to-Start, Start-to-Start, etc.) define how tasks relate to one another.
- Proper sequencing organizes tasks in the correct order and ensures workflow accuracy.
- Use lead and lag times to fine-tune task schedules and accommodate project needs.
- Regularly review and update dependencies to maintain schedule integrity.

In the next chapter, we'll explore how to incorporate task constraints to add flexibility or enforce specific requirements in your project schedule.

Incorporating Task Constraints

Task constraints are an essential feature in Microsoft Project that allow you to control the scheduling of tasks by setting specific rules for when they must start or finish. Constraints can provide flexibility or enforce strict scheduling requirements, depending on your project's needs. This chapter explores the different types of task constraints, when to use them, and how to apply them effectively in your project plan.

1. Understanding Task Constraints

Task constraints are rules that limit the start or finish dates of tasks. They can either allow flexibility within the project schedule or enforce strict deadlines, depending on the type of constraint applied.

1.1 Why Use Task Constraints?

- To align tasks with external factors, such as stakeholder dependencies or resource availability.
- To ensure tasks adhere to project deadlines or milestone dates.
- To manage scheduling conflicts and maintain project timelines.

1.2 Types of Task Constraints

Microsoft Project supports eight types of task constraints, divided into three categories:

1. **Flexible Constraints**: Allow Microsoft Project to adjust task dates as needed.
   - **As Soon As Possible (ASAP)**: Default for most tasks; tasks start as early as possible.
   - **As Late As Possible (ALAP)**: Tasks are delayed as much as possible without impacting the project's end date.
2. **Semi-Flexible Constraints**: Allow some flexibility but require adherence to specific conditions.
   - **Start No Earlier Than (SNET)**: Task cannot start before a specified date.
   - **Finish No Earlier Than (FNET)**: Task cannot finish before a specified date.
   - **Start No Later Than (SNLT)**: Task must start by a specified date.
   - **Finish No Later Than (FNLT)**: Task must finish by a specified date.
3. **Inflexible Constraints**: Enforce strict start or finish dates.
   - **Must Start On (MSO)**: Task must start on a specific date.
   - **Must Finish On (MFO)**: Task must finish on a specific date.

2. Applying Task Constraints

Step 1: Select the Task

1. Open your project file and go to the **Gantt Chart View**.
2. Click on the task you want to constrain.

Step 2: Open Task Information

1. Right-click the task and select **Information**, or go to **Task > Task Information**.
2. Navigate to the **Advanced** tab.

Step 3: Set the Constraint Type and Date

1. Choose a constraint type from the **Constraint Type** dropdown menu.
2. If required, enter a **Constraint Date** (e.g., SNET with a date of 01/15/2025).

3. Click **OK** to apply the constraint.

---

3. Flexible Constraints

Flexible constraints are ideal for most tasks as they allow the schedule to adjust dynamically based on dependencies and resource availability.

Use Case: As Soon As Possible (ASAP)

- A task can begin immediately after its predecessors are complete.
- Example: If Task A finishes early, Task B starts early as well.

Use Case: As Late As Possible (ALAP)

- A task starts as late as possible while still meeting the project's deadline.
- Example: Use ALAP for non-critical tasks to optimize resource allocation.

---

4. Semi-Flexible Constraints

Semi-flexible constraints strike a balance between flexibility and control, ensuring certain conditions are met without being overly restrictive.

Use Case: Start No Earlier Than (SNET)

- A task cannot begin before a specified date.
- Example: A task dependent on the delivery of materials arriving on 03/01/2025.

Use Case: Finish No Later Than (FNLT)

- A task must finish by a specified date to avoid delays in subsequent tasks.
- Example: Completing vendor negotiations by 02/15/2025 to start production.

---

5. Inflexible Constraints

Inflexible constraints enforce hard deadlines and are best used sparingly to avoid limiting schedule flexibility.

Use Case: Must Start On (MSO)

- A task must start on a fixed date, regardless of dependencies.
- Example: A launch event scheduled for 04/01/2025.

Use Case: Must Finish On (MFO)

- A task must finish on a fixed date, ensuring no delays in final deliverables.
- Example: Submitting a regulatory compliance report by 06/30/2025.

---

6. Viewing and Managing Constraints

6.1 Display Constraints in the Gantt Chart

1. Add the **Constraint Type** and **Constraint Date** columns to the table:
   - Right-click the column header in the task table.
   - Select **Insert Column** and choose **Constraint Type** or **Constraint Date**.

6.2 Review Constraints in the Task Inspector

1. Highlight a task and click **Task > Inspect Task**.
2. The Task Inspector panel displays information about constraints, dependencies, and scheduling issues.

---

7. Tips for Effective Use of Task Constraints

1. **Use Flexible Constraints Whenever Possible**: Rely on ASAP or ALAP for most tasks to maintain schedule adaptability.
2. **Apply Semi-Flexible Constraints Strategically**: Use SNET or FNLT to align with external dependencies.
3. **Limit Inflexible Constraints**: Avoid overusing MSO or MFO, as they can create scheduling conflicts.
4. **Document Constraints**: Record the rationale for constraints to ensure transparency and consistency.
5. **Regularly Review Constraints**: Update or remove constraints as project conditions evolve.

---

8. Troubleshooting Constraint Issues

Problem: Tasks are not rescheduling automatically.

- **Solution**: Check for inflexible constraints (e.g., MSO or MFO) limiting flexibility.

Problem: Scheduling conflicts with dependent tasks.

- **Solution**: Review the Constraint Type and adjust dependencies as needed.

Problem: Task dates don't align with the project timeline.

- **Solution**: Verify that constraints are appropriate and do not conflict with task dependencies.

---

9. Summary

Task constraints are a powerful tool in Microsoft Project, allowing you to manage task scheduling with precision. By understanding the types of constraints and their appropriate use cases, you can create a balanced schedule that meets project requirements while maintaining flexibility.

Key Takeaways

- Constraints control when tasks can start or finish, based on project needs.
- Flexible constraints (ASAP, ALAP) are ideal for most tasks, while semi-flexible and inflexible constraints should be used selectively.
- Regularly review constraints to ensure they align with project goals and do not create unnecessary conflicts.

In the next chapter, we'll discuss defining milestones, a critical step in tracking progress and ensuring project success.

Defining Milestones

Milestones are a critical aspect of project planning. They represent significant points or achievements in a project and are used to measure progress, manage expectations, and provide stakeholders with a clear understanding of key deliverables. This chapter will guide you through the process of defining and incorporating milestones into your Microsoft Project plan.

1. Understanding Milestones

1.1 What Are Milestones?

- Milestones are tasks with **zero duration** that mark important events, deadlines, or achievements.
- They help highlight key points in the project schedule, such as the completion of a phase or the delivery of a critical component.

1.2 Importance of Milestones

- **Progress Tracking**: Monitor progress against significant goals.
- **Communication**: Provide clear checkpoints for stakeholders.
- **Risk Management**: Identify delays or issues early by monitoring milestone deadlines.
- **Project Phases**: Define transitions between project phases or major deliverables.

2. Defining Milestones in Microsoft Project

Step 1: Add a Milestone

1. Open your project in the **Gantt Chart View**.
2. Enter the milestone name in the **Task Name** column.
3. Set the **Duration** to **0 days**.
    - Microsoft Project automatically treats tasks with zero duration as milestones.
4. Press **Enter**, and the milestone will appear as a diamond symbol in the Gantt Chart.

Step 2: Convert an Existing Task to a Milestone

1. Select the task you want to convert.
2. In the **Duration** column, change the value to **0 days**.
3. The task will now display as a milestone.

3. Associating Milestones with Tasks

3.1 Linking Milestones to Predecessors and Successors

Milestones can be linked to other tasks to create dependencies.

1. Highlight the milestone and the task you want to link.
2. Click **Task > Schedule > Link Tasks**.
    - For example, link the "Phase Completion" milestone to the last task in a phase.

3.2 Using Milestones to Mark Phase Completion

- Create a milestone at the end of a group of tasks to indicate the completion of that phase.

- Link the milestone to the final task in the phase.

4. Assigning Dates to Milestones

Milestones can either inherit their dates from dependencies or be assigned specific dates.

4.1 Automatic Scheduling of Milestones

- By default, milestone dates are determined by their linked predecessors.
- For example, if a milestone is linked to the end of a task, it will automatically align with that task's finish date.

4.2 Manually Setting Milestone Dates

1. Select the milestone in the **Task Name** column.
2. Enter a specific start or finish date in the **Start** or **Finish** column.
   - Use this method when the milestone date is fixed, such as a regulatory deadline.

5. Using Milestones in Reports and Dashboards

5.1 Highlighting Milestones in Reports

- Milestones are automatically included in standard reports, such as **Milestone Reports**.
- To generate a milestone-specific report:
  1. Navigate to **Report > New Report > Chart or Table**.
  2. Filter the report to display only milestones.

5.2 Tracking Milestones in Dashboards

- Use the **Timeline View** to add milestones for a high-level overview.
- Customize the Gantt Chart to highlight milestone symbols for better visibility.

6. Tips for Effective Milestone Management

1. **Align with Key Deliverables**: Ensure milestones correspond to critical project deliverables or decision points.
2. **Limit the Number of Milestones**: Use milestones sparingly to avoid cluttering the project schedule.
3. **Communicate Milestone Dates**: Share milestone dates with stakeholders to manage expectations.
4. **Monitor Milestones Regularly**: Review milestones during progress updates to ensure the project stays on track.
5. **Link Milestones to Dependencies**: Avoid floating milestones by linking them to relevant tasks.

7. Common Issues and Troubleshooting

Problem: Milestones not appearing in the Gantt Chart.

- **Solution**: Ensure the duration is set to **0 days** and check the display settings in the Gantt Chart view.

Problem: Milestone dates do not align with task dependencies.

- **Solution**: Verify the task links and adjust dependencies to reflect accurate scheduling.

Problem: Stakeholders misunderstand milestone significance.

- **Solution**: Clearly define and communicate the purpose of each milestone in project documentation.

---

8. Summary

Milestones play a vital role in project planning by marking significant events and providing clear progress indicators. By incorporating milestones effectively in Microsoft Project, you can enhance communication, track progress, and manage project timelines more efficiently.

Key Takeaways

- Milestones are zero-duration tasks that represent key events or deliverables.
- Use milestones to mark phase transitions, deadlines, or critical achievements.
- Link milestones to dependencies for accurate scheduling and tracking.
- Regularly review and update milestones to ensure alignment with project goals.

In the next section, we'll start with resource management essentials. Let's continue!

Section IV:
Resource Management Essentials

Introducing Resource Types

Resources are an essential part of any project plan, as they represent the people, equipment, and materials required to complete tasks. In Microsoft Project, understanding and correctly categorizing resource types is the first step in effective resource management. This chapter introduces the three primary resource types and explores how they are used to allocate and track project needs efficiently.

1. Overview of Resource Types in Microsoft Project

Microsoft Project categorizes resources into three main types:

1. **Work Resources**: Represent the people or equipment that perform tasks.
2. **Material Resources**: Represent consumable items used during the project.
3. **Cost Resources**: Represent financial expenditures, such as travel or overhead costs, that are not directly tied to work or materials.

Why Understanding Resource Types is Important

- Enables accurate resource allocation and tracking.
- Prevents resource conflicts and overallocations.
- Facilitates realistic scheduling and budgeting.

2. Work Resources

Work resources represent the effort required to complete tasks. They can include individuals, teams, or equipment that actively contribute to task execution.

Key Characteristics of Work Resources

- Measured in **time units** (e.g., hours, days, weeks).
- Have availability and cost rates that affect project schedules and budgets.
- Can be assigned to multiple tasks simultaneously, depending on availability.

Examples of Work Resources

- **People**: Project managers, engineers, designers, developers.
- **Equipment**: Machines, tools, or devices used to perform work.

Setting Up Work Resources

1. Go to **View > Resource Sheet**.
2. Enter the resource name in the **Resource Name** column.
3. Select **Work** in the **Type** column.
4. Define availability and cost rates in the corresponding columns.

3. Material Resources

Material resources represent physical items or supplies that are consumed during the project. Unlike work resources, they are not associated with time units.

Key Characteristics of Material Resources

- Measured in **units** (e.g., liters, tons, units).
- Have fixed costs per unit.
- Do not have availability limits, as they are typically procured as needed.

Examples of Material Resources

- Construction materials: Concrete, steel, bricks.
- Office supplies: Paper, ink cartridges, cables.
- Manufacturing items: Raw materials, chemicals, components.

Setting Up Material Resources

1. Go to **View > Resource Sheet**.
2. Enter the resource name in the **Resource Name** column.
3. Select **Material** in the **Type** column.
4. Specify the unit of measurement (e.g., "ton," "box") in the **Material Label** column.
5. Define the cost per unit in the **Standard Rate** column.

4. Cost Resources

Cost resources represent financial expenses that are not directly tied to work or materials. They allow you to track specific costs, such as travel, training, or consultancy fees, without linking them to time or quantity.

Key Characteristics of Cost Resources

- Have no time or quantity component.
- Used to capture additional expenses in the project budget.
- Are assigned to tasks to represent one-time or recurring costs.

Examples of Cost Resources

- Travel expenses: Flights, accommodation, car rentals.
- Fees: Licenses, permits, consultancy charges.
- Overheads: Administrative costs, utilities.

Setting Up Cost Resources

1. Go to **View > Resource Sheet**.
2. Enter the resource name in the **Resource Name** column.
3. Select **Cost** in the **Type** column.

5. Resource Attributes and Settings

Regardless of the resource type, there are several key attributes to configure for effective management:

5.1 Resource Name

- Enter a descriptive name for the resource (e.g., "John Smith," "Excavator," "Steel").

5.2 Initials

- Assign initials to identify resources easily in task assignments and reports.

5.3 Max Units

- For work resources, define the maximum capacity available (e.g., 100% for full-time availability, 50% for part-time).

5.4 Standard and Overtime Rates

- Specify hourly rates for work resources or cost per unit for material resources.
- Enter overtime rates for work resources to account for additional costs.

5.5 Availability Dates

- Set start and end dates for resource availability if the resource is only available for a specific duration.

---

6. Assigning Resources to Tasks

Once resources are set up, you can assign them to tasks to ensure proper allocation and scheduling.

How to Assign Resources

1. Select the task in the **Gantt Chart View**.
2. Click **Task > Assign Resources** or use the **Resource Names** column.
3. Choose the resource from the list and specify the units or quantity.

---

7. Best Practices for Managing Resource Types

1. **Define Resources Early**: Set up resource types at the start of the project to streamline task assignments.
2. **Use Descriptive Names**: Clearly name resources to avoid confusion during assignment and reporting.
3. **Track Costs Accurately**: Ensure cost rates and material quantities are entered correctly to maintain budget accuracy.
4. **Monitor Availability**: Regularly review resource availability to avoid overallocations or shortages.
5. **Leverage Resource Types**: Use cost and material resources effectively to capture all aspects of project expenses.

---

8. Common Issues and Troubleshooting

Problem: Resource not available for assignment.

- **Solution**: Check the resource's availability dates and maximum units in the Resource Sheet.

Problem: Incorrect cost calculations.

- **Solution**: Verify the standard and overtime rates for work resources or cost per unit for material resources.

Problem: Material quantities not reflected correctly.

- **Solution**: Ensure the correct unit of measurement is entered in the Material Label column.

---

9. Summary

Understanding resource types is the foundation of effective resource management in Microsoft Project. By categorizing resources as work, material, or cost types and configuring their attributes appropriately, you can ensure accurate allocation, scheduling, and cost tracking.

Key Takeaways

- **Work Resources**: Represent people or equipment performing tasks, measured in time units.
- **Material Resources**: Represent consumable items, measured in units.
- **Cost Resources**: Represent financial expenses unrelated to time or quantities.
- Configure resource attributes such as availability, cost rates, and units for accurate project planning.

In the next chapter, we'll explore how to add and edit resources in Microsoft Project, enabling you to refine your resource pool as your project evolves.

Adding and Editing Resources

Effective resource management begins with accurately adding and editing resources in Microsoft Project. Resources represent the people, materials, and costs required to complete your project tasks. This chapter provides a step-by-step guide on how to add and edit resources, ensuring your project is well-equipped and organized for success.

1. Accessing the Resource Sheet

The **Resource Sheet** is the primary view for adding, editing, and managing resources in Microsoft Project.

Step 1: Open the Resource Sheet

1. Go to **View > Resource Sheet**.
2. The Resource Sheet displays a table where you can enter and modify resource details.

Step 2: Understand the Resource Sheet Columns

The key columns in the Resource Sheet include:

- **Resource Name**: The name of the resource (e.g., person, equipment, material).
- **Type**: The resource type (Work, Material, or Cost).
- **Material Label**: The unit of measurement for material resources.
- **Max Units**: The maximum availability of the resource.
- **Standard Rate**: The cost per time unit (e.g., per hour for work resources).
- **Overtime Rate**: The additional cost for overtime work.
- **Cost/Use**: Fixed costs per use of the resource.
- **Group**: The category or team the resource belongs to.

2. Adding Resources

2.1 Adding Work Resources

1. In the Resource Sheet, enter the name of the resource in the **Resource Name** column.
2. Set the **Type** to **Work**.
3. Define the **Max Units**:
   - Enter **100%** for a full-time resource.
   - Enter **50%** for a part-time resource.
4. Specify the **Standard Rate** (e.g., $50/hour).
5. Enter the **Overtime Rate** if applicable (e.g., $75/hour).

2.2 Adding Material Resources

1. In the Resource Sheet, enter the name of the material in the **Resource Name** column (e.g., "Steel," "Concrete").
2. Set the **Type** to **Material**.
3. Enter the unit of measurement in the **Material Label** column (e.g., "ton," "box").
4. Specify the **Standard Rate** for the material (e.g., $100/ton).

2.3 Adding Cost Resources

1. Enter the name of the cost resource in the **Resource Name** column (e.g., "Travel," "Consulting").

2. Set the **Type** to **Cost**.

3. Editing Resources

You can update resource details at any time to reflect changes in availability, costs, or other attributes.

3.1 Editing Resource Information

1. Select the resource you want to edit in the Resource Sheet.
2. Right-click the resource and choose **Information**, or click **Resource > Information**.
3. In the **Resource Information** dialog box, update the following:
   - **Resource Type**: Change between Work, Material, or Cost.
   - **Availability**: Adjust the availability dates and maximum units.
   - **Costs**: Modify the standard rate, overtime rate, or cost per use.
4. Click **OK** to save changes.

3.2 Adjusting Resource Availability

1. Open the **Resource Information** dialog box.
2. Go to the **General** tab.
3. Under **Resource Availability**, specify the start and end dates and the corresponding maximum units.

4. Importing Resources from External Sources

If your organization maintains resource data in other tools like Excel or databases, you can import it into Microsoft Project.

Step 1: Prepare the Resource Data

1. Ensure the external data includes columns for resource attributes, such as name, type, and rates.
2. Save the file in a supported format (e.g., .xlsx or .csv).

Step 2: Import the Data

1. Go to **File > Open** and select your resource file.
2. Use the **Import Wizard** to map columns from the external file to fields in the Resource Sheet.

5. Tips for Managing Resources

1. **Use Descriptive Names**: Clearly name resources to avoid confusion during assignment and tracking.
2. **Group Resources**: Categorize resources by teams, departments, or functions using the **Group** column.
3. **Track Costs Accurately**: Regularly update rates and costs to reflect changes in budgets or contracts.
4. **Review Resource Availability**: Periodically check resource availability to prevent overallocations.
5. **Utilize the Resource Pool**: For large projects, create a shared resource pool to manage resources across multiple projects.

6. Common Issues and Troubleshooting

Problem: Resource not available for assignment.

- **Solution**: Check the **Max Units** and availability dates in the Resource Sheet.

Problem: Costs are not calculating correctly.

- **Solution**: Verify the **Standard Rate** and **Overtime Rate** values for the resource.

Problem: Imported resources missing critical details.

- **Solution**: Ensure all required columns are correctly mapped during the import process.

---

7. Summary

Adding and editing resources in Microsoft Project is a fundamental step in managing your project effectively. By accurately defining resource details, you can ensure proper allocation, availability, and cost tracking.

Key Takeaways

- Use the Resource Sheet to add and manage work, material, and cost resources.
- Regularly update resource details to reflect changes in availability or costs.
- Leverage external data sources to import resources and streamline setup.
- Monitor resource attributes like availability and costs to maintain project accuracy.

In the next chapter, we'll discuss assigning resources to tasks, a critical step in building a realistic project schedule and managing workloads effectively.

Assigning Resources to Tasks

Assigning resources to tasks in Microsoft Project is a critical step in creating a realistic project schedule. It ensures that the necessary people, equipment, or materials are allocated appropriately to complete tasks within the specified time and budget. This chapter provides a detailed guide on how to assign resources to tasks effectively and avoid common pitfalls.

1. Why Assign Resources to Tasks?

1.1 Accurate Scheduling

- Assigning resources ensures that task durations and schedules reflect real-world constraints.

1.2 Effective Workload Management

- Prevents overloading team members or resources by tracking their availability and workload.

1.3 Budget Tracking

- Calculates project costs based on resource rates, helping manage the budget effectively.

2. Steps to Assign Resources to Tasks

Step 1: Open the Task View

1. Switch to the **Gantt Chart View** or **Task Usage View** for detailed task management.

Step 2: Open the Assign Resources Dialog Box

1. Select the task you want to assign a resource to.
2. Navigate to **Task > Assign Resources** or press **Alt + F10**.
3. The **Assign Resources** dialog box will appear, showing a list of available resources.

Step 3: Assign Resources

1. Select the resource(s) from the list.
2. Specify the **Units** (percentage of the resource's availability) to assign:
   - Example: Assign **50%** for part-time work or **100%** for full-time.
3. Click **Assign** to allocate the resource to the selected task.

3. Managing Resource Assignments

3.1 Adjusting Resource Workload

After assigning resources, you may need to adjust their workload:

1. Go to the **Task Usage View** or **Resource Usage View**.
2. Modify the **Work** column to adjust the hours assigned to each resource.

3.2 Assigning Multiple Resources to a Single Task

- Assign multiple resources to a task to split the work:

- Example: Assign two engineers to a task requiring 40 hours of work, with each contributing 20 hours.
- Use the **Effort-Driven** setting to control how work is distributed among resources.

---

4. Assigning Material Resources to Tasks

4.1 Assigning Quantities

1. Select the task and open the **Assign Resources** dialog box.
2. Select a **Material Resource** from the list.
3. Enter the quantity of material required (e.g., 10 tons of concrete) in the **Units** field.
4. Click **Assign** to complete the allocation.

---

5. Assigning Cost Resources to Tasks

Cost resources represent financial expenses not tied to time or materials:

1. Select the task and open the **Assign Resources** dialog box.
2. Choose the **Cost Resource** from the list.
3. Click **Assign**, then:
   - Go to the **Task Usage View**.
   - Enter the cost value directly in the **Cost** column.

---

6. Understanding Effort-Driven Scheduling

Effort-driven scheduling is a feature that redistributes work when resources are added or removed from a task.

6.1 How It Works

- Total work remains constant, but individual resource workloads adjust.
- Example: If a task requires 40 hours of work and one resource is assigned, they will handle all 40 hours. Adding a second resource splits the work into 20 hours each.

6.2 Enabling or Disabling Effort-Driven Scheduling

1. Select the task and go to **Task > Information**.
2. In the **Advanced** tab, check or uncheck **Effort Driven**.

---

7. Using Task Types for Assignments

Task types determine how changes to work, duration, or resource assignments affect scheduling.

7.1 Task Type Options

1. **Fixed Units**: Changes to work or duration adjust the other, but resource units remain constant.
2. **Fixed Work**: Changes to duration adjust the units, keeping work constant.
3. **Fixed Duration**: Changes to work adjust the units, keeping duration constant.

7.2 Setting Task Types

1. Select the task and go to **Task > Information**.
2. In the **Advanced** tab, choose the desired **Task Type**.

---

8. Monitoring Resource Assignments

8.1 Use the Resource Usage View

1. Go to **View > Resource Usage**.
2. Check the allocation of resources across tasks to identify overallocations or underutilization.

8.2 Resolving Overallocations

1. Identify overallocated resources in the **Resource Sheet** or **Resource Usage View** (marked in red).
2. Adjust task durations, reassign resources, or level workloads to resolve conflicts.

---

9. Tips for Effective Resource Assignment

1. **Plan Resource Availability**: Ensure resource calendars reflect holidays, part-time schedules, or other constraints.
2. **Use Groups for Large Teams**: Organize resources into groups for easier allocation (e.g., "Engineering Team").
3. **Leverage Task Types**: Choose task types that align with your project's scheduling needs.
4. **Communicate Assignments**: Share resource assignments with team members to manage expectations.
5. **Regularly Monitor Assignments**: Periodically review resource allocation to prevent overloading or idle time.

---

10. Common Issues and Troubleshooting

Problem: Resource Overallocation

- **Solution**: Use the Resource Leveling feature or adjust task dependencies and durations.

Problem: Resource Costs Not Calculating

- **Solution**: Verify that the resource's standard and overtime rates are entered correctly in the Resource Sheet.

Problem: Material Quantities Incorrect

- **Solution**: Check the **Units** field when assigning material resources to tasks.

---

11. Summary

Assigning resources to tasks ensures your project plan is actionable, realistic, and efficient. By accurately allocating work, material, and cost resources, you can manage workloads, track budgets, and maintain schedules effectively.

Key Takeaways

- Use the **Assign Resources** dialog box to allocate resources to tasks.
- Adjust workloads and monitor resource usage to avoid overallocations.
- Leverage effort-driven scheduling and task types to control how assignments affect task durations.
- Regularly review resource allocations to ensure optimal utilization.

In the next chapter, we'll explore handling overallocations, providing strategies to balance workloads and ensure your project runs smoothly.

Handling Overallocations

Resource overallocation occurs when a resource is assigned more work than their available capacity, which can lead to delays, reduced efficiency, or burnout. Handling overallocations effectively in Microsoft Project is crucial for maintaining a balanced workload and ensuring project success. This chapter explores techniques and tools to identify, analyze, and resolve overallocations.

1. What Is Resource Overallocation?

1.1 Definition

Overallocation happens when a resource's assigned work exceeds their available capacity during a specific time period.

1.2 Common Causes of Overallocations

- Assigning a resource to multiple tasks simultaneously.
- Unrealistic task durations or workloads.
- Failure to account for non-working time or part-time availability.

2. Identifying Overallocations

2.1 Resource Sheet View

1. Navigate to **View > Resource Sheet**.
2. Overallocated resources are highlighted in **red**.

2.2 Resource Usage View

1. Go to **View > Resource Usage**.
2. Check the **Work** column against the **Max Units** column to identify discrepancies.

2.3 Team Planner View

1. Open the **Team Planner** view (**View > Team Planner**).
2. Overallocated tasks are marked with **red bars** under the resource's timeline.

3. Resolving Overallocations

3.1 Adjust Task Assignments

1. Open the overallocated resource's assignments in the **Resource Usage View**.
2. Reassign some tasks to other available resources:
   - Select the task and open **Task > Assign Resources**.
   - Assign a new resource and reduce the units of the overallocated resource.

3.2 Leveling Resources

Resource leveling is an automated feature in Microsoft Project that resolves overallocations by adjusting task schedules.

How to Use Resource Leveling

1. Go to **Resource > Leveling Options**.
2. Configure the leveling settings:
    ○ **Automatic or Manual**: Choose how you want leveling applied.
    ○ **Level Only Within Available Slack**: Ensures leveling does not delay the project finish date.
    ○ **Level Entire Project**: Adjusts schedules across the entire project timeline.
3. Click **Level All** to apply changes.

3.3 Split Tasks

1. Select the overallocated task in the **Gantt Chart View**.
2. Go to **Task > Split Task**.
3. Drag the split bar to create gaps in the schedule, reducing workload for the overallocated resource.

3.4 Adjust Task Durations

1. Extend the task duration to spread the workload over a longer period:
    ○ Double-click the task to open **Task Information**.
    ○ Update the **Duration** field.
2. Microsoft Project recalculates work distribution automatically.

---

4. Preventing Overallocations

4.1 Set Accurate Resource Calendars

1. Go to **Resource > Change Working Time**.
2. Update resource calendars to reflect non-working days, part-time availability, or other constraints.

4.2 Use Max Units Effectively

- Define realistic maximum units for each resource in the **Resource Sheet** (e.g., 50% for part-time employees).

4.3 Monitor Resource Workload Regularly

- Use the **Resource Usage** or **Team Planner** views periodically to check for potential overallocations.

4.4 Prioritize Critical Tasks

- Assign overallocated resources to critical tasks first and defer non-critical work to reduce strain.

---

5. Advanced Techniques for Resolving Overallocations

5.1 Delay Task Start Dates

- Adjust task dependencies or manually set later start dates to reduce overlapping work.
1. Go to the **Gantt Chart View**.
2. Drag task bars to delay start dates or use the **Task Information** dialog box.

5.2 Break Down Tasks into Subtasks

- Divide large tasks into smaller components to distribute work more evenly among resources.

5.3 Optimize Task Dependencies

- Adjust task dependencies to allow parallel work:
  - Change **Finish-to-Start** dependencies to **Start-to-Start** where feasible.

5.4 Increase Resource Capacity

- Add additional resources to the project to share the workload:
  - Go to **Resource > Add Resources** and assign them to overallocated tasks.

---

6. Tips for Effective Overallocation Management

1. **Regular Monitoring**: Check resource workloads weekly or bi-weekly to catch overallocations early.
2. **Use Filters**: Apply the **Overallocated Resources** filter in the **Resource Sheet** to focus on problematic resources.
3. **Communicate Changes**: Inform team members of schedule adjustments to avoid misunderstandings.
4. **Review Dependencies**: Ensure task dependencies are logical and do not create unnecessary conflicts.
5. **Document Adjustments**: Keep a record of changes made to the schedule for future reference.

---

7. Common Issues and Troubleshooting

Problem: Resource Leveling Delays Critical Tasks

- **Solution**: Use the **Level Only Within Available Slack** option to limit delays.

Problem: Overallocated Resources Not Highlighted

- **Solution**: Ensure **Max Units** are set correctly for each resource in the **Resource Sheet**.

Problem: Task Splits Create Gaps in Workflow

- **Solution**: Review task dependencies and reschedule to minimize disruptions.

---

8. Summary

Handling overallocations is a vital aspect of resource management in Microsoft Project. By identifying overallocated resources, using leveling techniques, and making schedule adjustments, you can maintain a balanced workload and ensure the timely delivery of your project.

Key Takeaways

- Overallocations occur when a resource's workload exceeds its capacity.
- Use views like **Resource Sheet**, **Resource Usage**, and **Team Planner** to identify overallocations.
- Resolve overallocations through resource leveling, reassignments, task splitting, or duration adjustments.
- Prevent overallocations by setting accurate resource calendars, monitoring workloads, and prioritizing critical tasks.

In the next chapter, we'll explore how to set project baselines, a critical step in tracking project performance and measuring progress against the original plan.

Section V:
Scheduling and Baselines

Setting Project Baselines

Setting a baseline in Microsoft Project is a crucial step in tracking and managing your project. A baseline is essentially a snapshot of your project plan at a specific point in time, capturing the original schedule, costs, and scope. It serves as a reference point for comparing actual progress and performance against the initial plan. This chapter provides a comprehensive guide on how to set, manage, and utilize baselines effectively in Microsoft Project.

1. What Is a Project Baseline?

A project baseline includes three key elements:

- **Schedule Baseline**: The planned start and finish dates of tasks.
- **Cost Baseline**: The budgeted costs for tasks, resources, and the overall project.
- **Scope Baseline**: The planned deliverables and tasks required to complete the project.

Why Set a Baseline?

- **Performance Tracking**: Compare actual progress against the original plan.
- **Stakeholder Communication**: Provide a clear benchmark for reporting and decision-making.
- **Change Management**: Evaluate the impact of changes on the project's scope, timeline, and budget.

2. When to Set a Baseline

1. **After Finalizing the Project Plan**: Set a baseline once all tasks, resources, and schedules are confirmed.
2. **Before Project Execution**: Ensure the baseline reflects the initial plan before work begins.
3. **After Major Updates**: If significant changes occur, save a new baseline to track progress against the revised plan.

3. Setting a Baseline in Microsoft Project

Step 1: Finalize Your Project Plan

1. Ensure all tasks, durations, dependencies, and resource assignments are accurate.
2. Review the project timeline and budget to confirm they align with objectives.

Step 2: Access the Baseline Feature

1. Go to **Project > Set Baseline**.
2. Select **Set Baseline** from the dropdown menu.

Step 3: Choose the Baseline to Save

1. In the **Set Baseline** dialog box, select **Baseline** to save the plan as the primary baseline.
   ○ Microsoft Project allows up to 11 baselines (Baseline and Baseline 1 through Baseline 10).
2. Choose whether to save the baseline for the entire project or specific tasks.

Step 4: Confirm and Save

1. Click **OK** to save the baseline.
2. Microsoft Project stores the baseline data, including start/finish dates, durations, costs, and work.

---

4. Viewing Baseline Data

4.1 Use the Gantt Chart View

1. Add baseline columns to the task table:
   ○ Right-click a column header, select **Insert Column**, and choose fields like **Baseline Start**, **Baseline Finish**, or **Baseline Cost**.
2. Compare baseline values with current task data.

4.2 Use the Tracking Gantt View

1. Navigate to **View > Tracking Gantt**.
2. Baseline bars appear below the task bars, showing planned vs. actual progress.

---

5. Updating and Managing Baselines

5.1 Re-Baselining the Project

If the project undergoes significant changes, update the baseline:

1. Go to **Project > Set Baseline**.
2. Choose an unused baseline (e.g., Baseline 1) to preserve the original baseline for reference.
3. Save the updated plan as the new baseline.

5.2 Clearing a Baseline

To remove baseline data:

1. Go to **Project > Clear Baseline**.
2. Select the baseline to clear and confirm your choice.

---

6. Using Baselines for Performance Tracking

6.1 Compare Planned vs. Actual Progress

1. Add **Variance** columns (e.g., **Start Variance**, **Finish Variance**) to the task table.
   ○ Variance shows the difference between baseline and actual dates or costs.
2. Use these columns to identify tasks that are ahead, on track, or behind schedule.

6.2 Monitor Key Metrics

1. **Baseline Cost vs. Actual Cost**: Track budget performance.

2. **Baseline Work vs. Actual Work**: Measure resource utilization.
3. **Baseline Duration vs. Actual Duration**: Identify schedule deviations.

---

7. Best Practices for Managing Baselines

1. **Set the Baseline Early**: Finalize and save the baseline before starting project execution.
2. **Use Multiple Baselines**: Save updated plans as new baselines to maintain a record of changes.
3. **Communicate Baseline Changes**: Inform stakeholders about re-baselining to maintain transparency.
4. **Review Variances Regularly**: Monitor baseline comparisons to identify and address issues promptly.
5. **Document Major Changes**: Record the reasons for re-baselining to track project history.

---

8. Troubleshooting Common Issues

Problem: Baseline data is missing.

- **Solution**: Confirm that a baseline was set for the entire project or the specific tasks.

Problem: Variance columns show incorrect values.

- **Solution**: Ensure that actual data (e.g., start/finish dates) is entered correctly and matches the project timeline.

Problem: Stakeholders question baseline changes.

- **Solution**: Maintain a clear log of baseline updates and the rationale behind them.

---

9. Summary

Setting project baselines is a critical step in managing and tracking your project effectively. A well-defined baseline provides a benchmark for measuring performance, managing changes, and ensuring project success.

Key Takeaways

- A baseline captures the original project plan for schedule, cost, and scope.
- Use the **Set Baseline** feature to save and manage baseline data.
- Compare baseline data with actual progress to monitor variances.
- Regularly review and update baselines as needed to reflect significant project changes.

In the next chapter, we'll explore how to adjust task durations and dependencies to keep your project on track and aligned with its goals.

Adjusting Task Durations and Dependencies

Effective project management requires flexibility in adjusting task durations and dependencies to accommodate changes, resolve conflicts, and optimize the project timeline. This chapter provides a detailed guide on how to modify task durations and dependencies in Microsoft Project to ensure your schedule remains realistic and aligned with project goals.

---

1. Adjusting Task Durations

Task duration is the amount of time allocated for completing a task. Modifying durations is often necessary to reflect changes in work estimates, resource availability, or project priorities.

1.1 Understanding Task Durations

- **Original Duration**: The planned time for completing the task.
- **Actual Duration**: The time already spent on the task.
- **Remaining Duration**: The time still required to complete the task.

1.2 How to Adjust Task Durations

1. Open the **Gantt Chart View**.
2. Locate the task in the task table.
3. In the **Duration** column, enter the new duration value (e.g., "5d" for 5 days, "3h" for 3 hours).
4. Press **Enter**, and Microsoft Project will automatically recalculate the task's schedule.

1.3 Tips for Adjusting Durations

- Use realistic estimates based on historical data or team input.
- Avoid frequent changes to durations unless necessary, as it can disrupt the schedule.
- Monitor dependencies when adjusting durations, as changes may impact linked tasks.

---

2. Adjusting Task Dependencies

Dependencies define the relationship between tasks and dictate the sequence of execution. Adjusting dependencies is essential when project priorities, workflows, or task constraints change.

2.1 Types of Task Dependencies

1. **Finish-to-Start (FS)**: Task B starts only after Task A finishes (default dependency).
2. **Start-to-Start (SS)**: Task B starts at the same time as Task A.
3. **Finish-to-Finish (FF)**: Task B finishes at the same time as Task A.
4. **Start-to-Finish (SF)**: Task B starts before Task A finishes (rarely used).

2.2 Modifying Dependencies

1. Open the **Gantt Chart View** or **Task Dependency Diagram**.
2. Select the task whose dependency you want to modify.
3. Go to **Task > Information**, then select the **Predecessors** tab.
4. Change the dependency type in the **Type** column (e.g., FS to SS).
5. Add or remove predecessors as needed.

---

3. Adding Lag and Lead Times

Lag and lead times are adjustments applied to task dependencies to create gaps or overlaps between linked tasks.

3.1 Lag Time

- Adds a delay between the predecessor and successor tasks.
- Example: Waiting 2 days after "Paint Walls" before starting "Install Fixtures".

How to Add Lag Time:

1. Open the **Task Information** dialog box.
2. Go to the **Predecessors** tab.
3. In the **Lag** column, enter a positive value (e.g., "2d" for 2 days).

3.2 Lead Time

- Allows the successor task to start before the predecessor finishes.
- Example: Starting "Begin Marketing Campaign" 3 days before "Finalize Brochure" ends.

How to Add Lead Time:

1. Open the **Task Information** dialog box.
2. Go to the **Predecessors** tab.
3. In the **Lag** column, enter a negative value (e.g., "-3d" for 3 days).

---

4. Managing Constraints When Adjusting Tasks

Task constraints affect how durations and dependencies are adjusted. Common constraints include:

- **As Soon As Possible (ASAP)**: Tasks start immediately after predecessors finish.
- **Finish No Later Than (FNLT)**: Tasks must finish by a specific date.
- **Must Start On (MSO)**: Tasks must begin on a fixed date.

How to Adjust Constraints

1. Open the **Task Information** dialog box.
2. Go to the **Advanced** tab.
3. Select a new constraint type and enter a specific date if required.

---

5. Viewing and Monitoring Changes

5.1 Tracking Gantt View

- Use the **Tracking Gantt View** to compare baseline durations and dependencies with the updated schedule.

5.2 Add Key Columns

- Add columns such as **Predecessors**, **Successors**, and **Start/Finish Variance** to the task table for quick analysis.

---

6. Best Practices for Adjusting Task Durations and Dependencies

1. **Communicate Changes**: Notify team members and stakeholders about major schedule adjustments.
2. **Monitor Dependencies**: Review the entire dependency chain to identify potential ripple effects.
3. **Use Historical Data**: Base duration estimates on past project performance for better accuracy.
4. **Limit Manual Adjustments**: Allow Microsoft Project to calculate dates and durations based on dependencies whenever possible.
5. **Revalidate the Schedule**: After adjustments, ensure the schedule still aligns with project milestones and deadlines.

---

7. Common Issues and Troubleshooting

Problem: Task dates do not update after adjusting dependencies.

- **Solution**: Check for constraints or manually set dates that may override dependency rules.

Problem: Adjusted durations create scheduling conflicts.

- **Solution**: Use the **Task Inspector** to identify and resolve conflicts.

Problem: Lag or lead times are not applied correctly.

- **Solution**: Verify the **Lag** column values in the **Predecessors** tab of the **Task Information** dialog box.

---

8. Summary

Adjusting task durations and dependencies is an essential skill for maintaining an accurate and flexible project schedule. By understanding the impact of these changes on the overall timeline and dependencies, you can ensure that your project remains on track and adaptable to unforeseen challenges.

Key Takeaways

- Task durations define how long work will take, while dependencies establish task relationships.
- Adjust durations and dependencies to reflect changes in project priorities or constraints.
- Use lag and lead times to fine-tune task relationships.
- Monitor adjustments to ensure they align with project milestones and avoid scheduling conflicts.

In the next chapter, we'll dive into managing the critical path, a crucial component for identifying tasks that directly impact your project's completion date.

Managing the Critical Path

The critical path is the sequence of tasks that determines the minimum time required to complete a project. Understanding and managing the critical path is essential for ensuring that your project stays on schedule and that key milestones are achieved. This chapter provides a step-by-step guide to identifying and managing the critical path in Microsoft Project, along with tips for optimizing it.

1. Understanding the Critical Path

1.1 What Is the Critical Path?

- The critical path is the longest sequence of dependent tasks that must be completed on time for the project to finish as scheduled.
- Tasks on the critical path have **zero slack**, meaning any delay in these tasks will delay the entire project.

1.2 Why Is the Critical Path Important?

- It helps project managers focus on tasks that directly impact the project timeline.
- Identifying the critical path ensures proper allocation of resources and prioritization of tasks.
- Monitoring the critical path allows proactive management of potential delays.

2. Identifying the Critical Path in Microsoft Project

Step 1: Switch to the Gantt Chart View

1. Open your project file and navigate to **View > Gantt Chart**.

Step 2: Highlight the Critical Path

1. Go to **Format > Critical Tasks** in the Gantt Chart Tools tab.
2. Tasks on the critical path will appear highlighted (e.g., in red).

Step 3: Use the Task Path Feature

1. Select a task in the Gantt Chart.
2. Go to **Format > Task Path**, then choose **Critical Path** to display task dependencies and their impact on the timeline.

3. Managing the Critical Path

3.1 Adjusting Task Durations

- Shorten the duration of tasks on the critical path to reduce the overall project timeline.
- Example: If a critical task is estimated at 10 days, reduce it to 8 days by reallocating resources or improving efficiency.

3.2 Modifying Task Dependencies

- Adjust task dependencies to allow parallel work:
  - Change **Finish-to-Start (FS)** dependencies to **Start-to-Start (SS)** where feasible.

o Example: Allow "Testing" to begin while "Development" is still ongoing.

3.3 Adding or Removing Resources

- Assign additional resources to critical tasks to expedite completion.
- Reallocate resources from non-critical tasks to focus on the critical path.

---

4. Monitoring the Critical Path

4.1 Regularly Check for Changes

- As tasks progress, the critical path may shift to other sequences of tasks.
- Reevaluate the critical path after significant updates to the project schedule.

4.2 Use the Tracking Gantt View

1. Navigate to **View > Tracking Gantt**.
2. Compare baseline and actual progress to identify variances in critical path tasks.

4.3 Monitor Slack Values

1. Add the **Total Slack** column to the task table:
   o Right-click a column header, select **Insert Column**, and choose **Total Slack**.
2. Focus on tasks with zero or negative slack, as these are on the critical path.

---

5. Optimizing the Critical Path

5.1 Fast Tracking

- Perform tasks in parallel rather than sequentially to reduce the project duration.
- Example: Overlap "Foundation Construction" with "Structural Framing" where dependencies allow.

5.2 Crashing

- Allocate additional resources to critical tasks to complete them faster.
- Consider the trade-offs between additional costs and reduced project duration.

5.3 Prioritizing Critical Tasks

- Ensure critical tasks are completed on time by prioritizing resources and attention.

---

6. Using Reports to Manage the Critical Path

6.1 Generate a Critical Path Report

1. Navigate to **Report > New Report > Task Report**.
2. Filter the report to include only critical tasks.

6.2 Include Critical Path in Stakeholder Updates

- Use critical path reports to communicate project risks and priorities with stakeholders.
- Highlight tasks that require immediate attention to avoid delays.

7. Common Issues and Troubleshooting

Problem: Critical Path Not Highlighted

- **Solution**: Ensure all tasks have dependencies and no tasks are manually scheduled.

Problem: Critical Path Keeps Changing

- **Solution**: Regularly update progress and evaluate task durations to reflect accurate dependencies.

Problem: Multiple Critical Paths

- **Solution**: Check the project settings to ensure that only the most critical sequence is highlighted, or manage each critical path separately.

8. Best Practices for Managing the Critical Path

1. **Keep Dependencies Logical**: Ensure task dependencies are realistic and necessary.
2. **Avoid Overloading Resources**: Allocate resources strategically to prevent bottlenecks.
3. **Review Regularly**: Monitor the critical path frequently, especially after updates or delays.
4. **Communicate with Teams**: Ensure all team members understand the importance of tasks on the critical path.
5. **Use Contingency Planning**: Identify alternative approaches to critical tasks in case of delays.

9. Summary

Managing the critical path is essential for delivering projects on time. By identifying critical tasks, monitoring their progress, and optimizing their execution, you can ensure your project stays on track and achieves its objectives.

Key Takeaways

- The critical path determines the minimum time required to complete a project.
- Use tools like the Gantt Chart, Task Path, and Tracking Gantt views to identify and manage the critical path.
- Apply techniques such as fast tracking and crashing to optimize the critical path and mitigate delays.
- Regularly review and adjust the critical path to reflect changes in the project.

In the next chapter, we'll explore balancing workloads, an essential step in managing resources effectively and ensuring smooth project execution.

Balancing Workloads

Balancing workloads is essential for ensuring that resources are utilized efficiently without being overburdened or underutilized. In Microsoft Project, balancing workloads involves redistributing tasks, adjusting assignments, and resolving overallocation issues. This chapter provides a comprehensive guide to identifying workload imbalances and using Microsoft Project's tools and techniques to address them.

1. What Is Workload Balancing?

Workload balancing ensures that resources are assigned tasks in a way that avoids overloading or periods of inactivity. The goal is to optimize resource utilization while maintaining the project schedule.

1.1 Importance of Balancing Workloads

- **Prevent Burnout**: Avoid overallocating resources, which can lead to fatigue and reduced productivity.
- **Maintain Efficiency**: Ensure resources are used effectively without idle time.
- **Ensure Timely Delivery**: Avoid delays caused by resource bottlenecks.

2. Identifying Workload Imbalances

2.1 Resource Sheet View

1. Navigate to **View > Resource Sheet**.
2. Overallocated resources are marked in **red**.

2.2 Resource Usage View

1. Go to **View > Resource Usage**.
2. Check the **Work** column to see the total hours assigned to each resource.
3. Compare the assigned hours to the resource's availability in the **Max Units** column.

2.3 Team Planner View

1. Open the **Team Planner** view (**View > Team Planner**).
2. Tasks assigned to overallocated resources appear as red bars in the timeline.

3. Techniques for Balancing Workloads

3.1 Adjusting Task Assignments

- Redistribute tasks from overallocated resources to underutilized ones.
1. Select the task in the **Gantt Chart View**.
2. Go to **Task > Assign Resources**.
3. Reassign the task to another resource or split the workload between multiple resources.

3.2 Changing Task Durations

- Extend task durations to reduce the daily workload on overallocated resources.
1. Double-click the task to open **Task Information**.
2. Adjust the **Duration** field to spread the work over a longer period.

3.3 Leveling Resources

- Resource leveling automatically adjusts task schedules to resolve overallocations.

Steps for Resource Leveling

1. Go to **Resource > Leveling Options**.
2. Configure the options:
   - **Automatic or Manual** leveling.
   - **Level Only Within Available Slack** to avoid delays in project deadlines.
3. Click **Level All** to apply the adjustments.

3.4 Splitting Tasks

- Split tasks into smaller segments to distribute the workload more evenly over time.
1. Select the task in the **Gantt Chart View**.
2. Go to **Task > Split Task**.
3. Drag the split bar to create gaps in the task timeline.

3.5 Adding Resources

- Assign additional resources to critical tasks to share the workload.
1. Open the **Assign Resources** dialog box.
2. Add new resources to the task and adjust their units.

---

4. Using Microsoft Project Tools for Balancing Workloads

4.1 Task Inspector

- The Task Inspector provides recommendations for resolving resource conflicts.
1. Select the task in the **Gantt Chart View**.
2. Click **Task > Inspect Task**.
3. Review the suggestions for resolving overallocations.

4.2 Work Contours

- Adjust work contours to distribute effort more evenly across the task duration.
1. Select the task and go to **Task Information > Resources**.
2. Choose a work contour (e.g., **Flat**, **Back Loaded**, **Front Loaded**, **Bell**).

4.3 Timescale View

- Use the Timescale View to visually monitor workloads across resources and time periods.
1. Go to **View > Resource Usage**.
2. Adjust the timescale to show workload distribution daily, weekly, or monthly.

---

5. Tips for Effective Workload Balancing

1. **Monitor Resource Availability**: Regularly review the **Max Units** and **Calendars** for each resource to account for non-working days and part-time schedules.
2. **Use Groups for Team Assignments**: Categorize resources by team or skill set to facilitate task reassignments.
3. **Prioritize Critical Tasks**: Allocate resources to tasks on the critical path first to avoid project delays.

4. **Communicate Changes**: Inform team members about schedule and assignment adjustments.
5. **Avoid Last-Minute Adjustments**: Balance workloads early to prevent disruptions to the project timeline.

---

6. Common Issues and Troubleshooting

Problem: Resource Leveling Delays Critical Tasks

- **Solution**: Use the **Level Only Within Available Slack** option to avoid impacting the project deadline.

Problem: Overallocated Resources Remain Unresolved

- **Solution**: Check for fixed task constraints that prevent scheduling adjustments.

Problem: Resource Assignments Are Not Balanced

- **Solution**: Use the **Resource Usage View** to identify underutilized resources and reassign tasks accordingly.

---

7. Summary

Balancing workloads is essential for maintaining a productive and efficient project environment. By identifying workload imbalances early and using Microsoft Project's tools to resolve them, you can ensure your resources are utilized effectively while keeping the project on track.

Key Takeaways

- Monitor resource workloads using views like **Resource Usage** and **Team Planner**.
- Adjust assignments, task durations, and dependencies to resolve overallocations.
- Use resource leveling and work contours to balance workloads automatically.
- Communicate and document changes to ensure transparency and alignment among team members.

In the next section, we'll learn how to track project progress efficiently using various Microsoft Project features.

Section VI:
Tracking Project Progress

Updating Tasks and Progress

Tracking progress is critical for ensuring that your project stays on schedule and within budget. Updating tasks in Microsoft Project helps you monitor how the project evolves and make informed decisions when deviations occur. This chapter focuses on the tools and techniques you can use to update tasks and track progress effectively.

1. Importance of Updating Tasks and Progress

1.1 Why Track Progress?

- **Monitor Performance**: Identify tasks that are on track, behind schedule, or ahead of schedule.
- **Maintain Accuracy**: Keep the project plan up-to-date with actual performance data.
- **Facilitate Decision-Making**: Use real-time data to make adjustments and ensure project success.

1.2 Key Progress Metrics

- **Percent Complete**: Indicates how much of the task has been finished.
- **Actual Start and Finish Dates**: Reflect when a task started or ended.
- **Actual Work**: Measures the number of hours or effort spent on a task.
- **Remaining Work**: Estimates the work left to complete the task.

2. Methods for Updating Tasks in Microsoft Project

Microsoft Project provides several methods to update tasks based on the level of detail required.

2.1 Using the Task Information Dialog Box

1. Double-click the task in the **Gantt Chart View**.
2. Go to the **General** tab.
3. Enter the actual start date, finish date, and percent complete.
4. Click **OK** to save updates.

2.2 Updating Directly in the Task Table

1. Add progress-related columns, such as **% Complete**, **Actual Start**, and **Actual Finish**, to the task table.
2. Enter updates directly in the corresponding cells.

2.3 Using the Update Tasks Feature

1. Select the task(s) to update.
2. Go to **Task > Schedule > Update Tasks**.
3. Specify the actual work completed or remaining work in the dialog box.

2.4 Using the Tracking Table

1. Switch to the **Tracking Table**:
   ○ Go to **View > Tables > Tracking**.
2. Update fields such as **Actual Start**, **Actual Finish**, **% Work Complete**, and **Remaining Work**.

---

3. Tracking Progress with Percent Complete

3.1 What Is Percent Complete?

- Represents the percentage of work completed for a task.

3.2 Updating Percent Complete

1. Go to the **Gantt Chart View** or **Task Sheet View**.
2. Locate the **% Complete** column.
3. Enter the updated value (e.g., "50%" for halfway done).

3.3 Visualizing Progress on the Gantt Chart

- Progress bars appear within the task bars to represent the percentage complete.

---

4. Updating Task Start and Finish Dates

4.1 Actual Start Date

- Reflects when a task actually began.
1. Double-click the task.
2. Enter the **Actual Start** date in the **General** tab.

4.2 Actual Finish Date

- Indicates when a task is completed.
1. Open the **Task Information** dialog box.
2. Enter the **Actual Finish** date.

---

5. Tracking Work and Effort

5.1 Updating Actual Work

1. Go to the **Resource Usage View** or **Task Usage View**.
2. Locate the **Actual Work** column.
3. Enter the number of hours or effort completed for the task.

5.2 Updating Remaining Work

1. In the same view, find the **Remaining Work** column.
2. Update the estimated hours or effort left to complete the task.

---

6. Automating Progress Updates

6.1 Status Date

- Use the status date to indicate the point in time for progress tracking.
1. Go to **Project > Status Date**.
2. Set the desired status date.

6.2 Reschedule Uncompleted Work

1. Go to **Project > Update Project**.
2. Select **Reschedule uncompleted work to start after [Status Date]**.
3. Apply changes to the entire project or specific tasks.

---

7. Monitoring Progress

7.1 Use the Tracking Gantt View

1. Navigate to **View > Tracking Gantt**.
2. Compare baseline task bars with progress bars to evaluate performance.

7.2 Apply Progress Lines

1. Go to **Format > Gridlines**.
2. Select **Progress Lines** and customize their appearance.
3. Progress lines highlight deviations from the planned schedule.

---

8. Tips for Effective Progress Updates

1. **Update Regularly**: Schedule updates weekly or biweekly to maintain accurate data.
2. **Use Baselines for Comparison**: Regularly compare actual progress against baseline data to track deviations.
3. **Communicate with Teams**: Ensure team members provide accurate updates on task progress.
4. **Focus on Critical Tasks**: Prioritize updating tasks on the critical path to avoid delays.
5. **Leverage Filters**: Use filters to focus on tasks that require updates or are behind schedule.

---

9. Common Issues and Troubleshooting

Problem: Progress Updates Do Not Reflect on the Schedule

- **Solution**: Ensure dependencies and constraints are correctly set. Update linked tasks as needed.

Problem: Percent Complete Shows Incorrect Values

- **Solution**: Verify the actual work and remaining work values for accuracy.

Problem: Task Bars Do Not Display Progress

- **Solution**: Check the **% Complete** field and ensure progress bars are enabled in the Gantt Chart settings.

---

10. Summary

Updating tasks and progress is a fundamental step in managing a project effectively. By regularly inputting actual data and tracking performance metrics, you can ensure your project remains on track and aligned with its goals.

Key Takeaways

- Use tools like the **Task Information** dialog box, **Tracking Table**, and **Gantt Chart View** to update progress.
- Track metrics such as **Percent Complete**, **Actual Work**, and **Remaining Work** for accurate performance monitoring.
- Leverage views like **Tracking Gantt** and progress lines for a visual representation of task updates.

In the next chapter, we'll explore monitoring percent complete in greater detail, including its impact on overall project performance and reporting.

Monitoring Percent Complete

Monitoring percent complete is a key aspect of tracking project progress in Microsoft Project. It provides a clear indication of how much work has been completed for each task and the overall project. This chapter explains how to effectively monitor percent complete, interpret its impact on the schedule, and use this information to keep your project on track.

1. Understanding Percent Complete

1.1 What Is Percent Complete?

- Percent complete is the proportion of work completed for a task, expressed as a percentage.
- For example, if a task requires 10 hours of work and 5 hours have been completed, it is 50% complete.

1.2 Why Monitor Percent Complete?

- **Track Progress**: Understand how much of the project is finished.
- **Identify Delays**: Spot tasks falling behind schedule.
- **Facilitate Communication**: Provide updates to stakeholders with quantifiable data.
- **Enable Adjustments**: Make informed decisions to reallocate resources or adjust timelines.

2. Methods for Monitoring Percent Complete

2.1 Using the Gantt Chart View

1. Open the **Gantt Chart View**.
2. Add the **% Complete** column:
    - Right-click a column header, select **Insert Column**, and choose **% Complete**.
3. Review the percent complete for each task.

2.2 Using the Task Usage View

1. Navigate to **View > Task Usage**.
2. Add the **% Complete** column to the table.
3. Monitor progress for each task and subtask.

2.3 Using the Tracking Table

1. Go to **View > Tables > Tracking**.
2. The **% Complete** field displays the progress for all tasks.

3. Updating Percent Complete

3.1 Manual Updates

1. Select the task in the **Gantt Chart View** or **Task Usage View**.
2. Enter the updated percent complete in the **% Complete** column.

3.2 Using the Task Information Dialog Box

1. Double-click the task to open the **Task Information** dialog box.
2. In the **General** tab, update the **% Complete** field.

3.3 Bulk Updates

1. Select multiple tasks.
2. Go to **Task > Mark on Track > Update Tasks**.
3. Specify the percent complete for the selected tasks.

---

4. Interpreting Percent Complete

4.1 Analyzing Progress

- **100% Complete**: Task is finished.
- **0% Complete**: Task has not started.
- **Partial Completion**: Reflects ongoing progress.

4.2 Identifying Discrepancies

Compare percent complete with the planned progress to identify tasks that are ahead, on track, or behind schedule.

4.3 Visualizing Percent Complete

- In the **Gantt Chart View**, progress bars within task bars visually represent the percent complete.
- Use the **Tracking Gantt View** to compare progress against the baseline schedule.

---

5. Monitoring Percent Complete for Groups and Phases

5.1 Summary Tasks

- Summary tasks automatically calculate percent complete based on their subtasks.
- Ensure subtasks are updated accurately to reflect progress for the phase.

5.2 Filtering for Key Tasks

1. Use filters to focus on critical tasks:
   - Go to **View > Filter > Critical Tasks**.
2. Monitor percent complete for these tasks to ensure milestones are met.

---

6. Using Reports for Monitoring Percent Complete

6.1 Built-In Reports

1. Navigate to **Report > In Progress**.
2. Use the report to view percent complete for tasks across the project.

6.2 Custom Reports

1. Go to **Report > New Report > Table Report**.
2. Include fields such as **Task Name**, **% Complete**, and **Finish Date**.

---

7. Best Practices for Monitoring Percent Complete

1. **Update Regularly**: Schedule updates weekly or biweekly to maintain accuracy.
2. **Use Realistic Estimates**: Ensure percent complete reflects actual progress, not optimistic projections.
3. **Communicate with Teams**: Confirm progress updates with team members to ensure accuracy.
4. **Leverage Visual Tools**: Use Gantt charts and tracking views to quickly assess task progress.
5. **Focus on Critical Tasks**: Prioritize monitoring for tasks on the critical path to avoid delays.

---

8. Common Issues and Troubleshooting

Problem: Percent Complete Does Not Reflect Actual Progress

- **Solution**: Verify actual work and remaining work values for accuracy.

Problem: Summary Task Percent Complete Is Incorrect

- **Solution**: Ensure all subtasks have been updated correctly.

Problem: Progress Bars Do Not Display on Gantt Chart

- **Solution**: Enable progress bars in the **Gantt Chart Tools > Format** menu.

---

9. Summary

Monitoring percent complete is an essential part of tracking project progress. By updating and reviewing percent complete regularly, project managers can ensure tasks are progressing as planned, identify delays, and make necessary adjustments to keep the project on track.

Key Takeaways

- Percent complete provides a clear measure of task and project progress.
- Use views like **Gantt Chart**, **Task Usage**, and **Tracking Table** to monitor and update percent complete.
- Leverage built-in reports for a comprehensive overview of progress.
- Ensure updates are accurate and align with actual work performed.

In the next chapter, we'll explore how to use timescales and time-phased data to analyze project progress and resource allocation in greater detail.

Using Timescales and Time-Phased Data

Effectively managing a project requires a detailed view of resource allocation, task progress, and cost distribution over time. Microsoft Project provides powerful tools to analyze timescales and time-phased data, enabling you to gain insights into project performance and make informed decisions. This chapter explores how to use these tools to track progress and optimize project outcomes.

1. Understanding Timescales and Time-Phased Data

1.1 What Are Timescales?

- Timescales represent the chronological breakdown of tasks, resources, and costs in a project.
- They can be customized to show data by day, week, month, quarter, or year.

1.2 What Is Time-Phased Data?

- Time-phased data breaks down information such as work, costs, and progress over a specific timescale.
- Example: Viewing how many hours a resource works daily or weekly on a task.

2. Configuring Timescales in Microsoft Project

2.1 Adjusting the Timescale View

1. Navigate to the **Gantt Chart View** or **Resource Usage View**.
2. Right-click the timescale bar at the top of the chart.
3. Select **Timescale** to open the customization options.

2.2 Setting Timescale Units

1. Choose the desired units (e.g., Days, Weeks, Months) for the timescale tiers.
2. Customize the format for each tier, such as displaying the week numbers or month abbreviations.

2.3 Using Multiple Tiers

- Microsoft Project allows up to three tiers (Top, Middle, and Bottom) to display detailed timescale information.
- Example: Use **Months** for the top tier and **Weeks** for the bottom tier for a comprehensive view.

3. Accessing Time-Phased Data

3.1 Resource Usage View

1. Go to **View > Resource Usage**.
2. The timescale grid displays work, costs, and availability for each resource over time.

3.2 Task Usage View

1. Navigate to **View > Task Usage**.
2. Review how work, costs, and progress are distributed across the timeline for each task.

3.3 Adding Time-Phased Data Columns

1. Right-click a column header in the timescale grid.
2. Choose fields such as **Work**, **Actual Work**, **Remaining Work**, or **Cost**.

---

4. Analyzing Time-Phased Data

4.1 Work Distribution

- Monitor how work is allocated to resources over time.
- Identify periods of overwork or underutilization using the **Work** field in the **Resource Usage View**.

4.2 Cost Tracking

- Review time-phased cost data to track expenditure trends.
- Use the **Cost** and **Actual Cost** fields to monitor budget usage over time.

4.3 Progress Monitoring

- Analyze progress with fields like **Actual Work** and **Remaining Work**.
- Use the **Tracking Gantt View** for a visual comparison of planned vs. actual progress.

---

5. Customizing Time-Phased Data for Better Insights

5.1 Filtering Data

1. Apply filters to focus on specific tasks or resources.
2. Example: Use the **Critical Tasks** filter to view time-phased data for tasks on the critical path.

5.2 Grouping Data

1. Go to **View > Group by** to organize time-phased data by criteria like resource type or task category.
2. Example: Group resources by department to analyze workload distribution.

5.3 Highlighting Key Metrics

- Add custom fields to highlight important metrics such as variance, delays, or cost overruns.

---

6. Using Reports to Summarize Timescales and Time-Phased Data

6.1 Built-In Reports

1. Navigate to **Report > Work Overview** or **Cost Overview**.
2. These reports provide summaries of time-phased work and cost data.

6.2 Custom Reports

1. Go to **Report > New Report > Table Report**.
2. Add fields such as **Work**, **Cost**, and **Baseline Work** to analyze trends over time.

---

7. Best Practices for Using Timescales and Time-Phased Data

1. **Choose Appropriate Timescales**: Adjust timescale units based on project duration and complexity.
   - Example: Use **Days** for short-term projects and **Weeks** for long-term projects.
2. **Monitor Regularly**: Review time-phased data weekly to identify and address potential issues.
3. **Focus on Critical Resources**: Analyze the workload of key resources to avoid overallocations.
4. **Leverage Visual Tools**: Use the **Resource Graph View** for a graphical representation of time-phased data.
5. **Communicate Trends**: Share time-phased insights with stakeholders to facilitate proactive decision-making.

---

8. Troubleshooting Common Issues

Problem: Timescale View Is Too Detailed or Too Broad

- **Solution**: Adjust the timescale units and tiers to suit your analysis needs.

Problem: Time-Phased Data Is Missing or Inaccurate

- **Solution**: Verify that actual data (e.g., work, cost) is entered for tasks and resources.

Problem: Overlapping Work or Costs

- **Solution**: Use resource leveling to resolve overallocations and redistribute workloads.

---

9. Summary

Timescales and time-phased data are powerful tools for understanding the chronological distribution of work, costs, and progress in a project. By leveraging Microsoft Project's features, you can gain valuable insights and make informed decisions to keep your project on track.

Key Takeaways

- Use timescales to view project data in different time units.
- Analyze time-phased data in the **Resource Usage** and **Task Usage** views.
- Customize timescales and data fields to focus on critical metrics.
- Use reports and visual tools to summarize and communicate findings.

In the next chapter, we'll explore how to review baseline vs. actual performance to measure project progress and assess alignment with initial plans.

Reviewing Baseline vs. Actual Performance

Reviewing baseline vs. actual performance is a critical aspect of project management that helps you understand how your project is progressing compared to the original plan. Microsoft Project provides robust tools to compare baseline data with actual performance metrics, enabling project managers to identify deviations, analyze trends, and take corrective actions. This chapter provides a detailed guide on how to effectively use these features.

1. Understanding Baseline and Actual Performance

1.1 What Is a Baseline?

- A baseline is a snapshot of your project's original plan, including task start and finish dates, durations, costs, and resource allocations.
- It serves as a reference point for measuring project performance.

1.2 What Is Actual Performance?

- Actual performance includes real-time data on task progress, resource usage, and costs as the project unfolds.

1.3 Why Compare Baseline vs. Actual Performance?

- **Identify Variances**: Spot deviations in schedule, cost, or scope.
- **Analyze Trends**: Understand factors contributing to project success or delays.
- **Facilitate Decision-Making**: Take corrective actions to realign the project with its goals.

2. Setting and Managing Baselines in Microsoft Project

2.1 Setting a Baseline

1. Go to **Project > Set Baseline > Set Baseline**.
2. Choose a baseline option (e.g., **Baseline 1, Baseline 2**) if you need multiple baselines for comparisons.
3. Click **OK** to save the baseline.

2.2 Updating the Baseline

- If significant changes occur, update the baseline to reflect the revised plan:
    1. Select **Project > Set Baseline**.
    2. Overwrite the existing baseline or save it as a new one.

3. Reviewing Baseline vs. Actual Performance

3.1 Using the Gantt Chart View

1. Switch to the **Tracking Gantt View**:
    - Go to **View > Tracking Gantt**.
2. Compare baseline task bars (gray) with actual progress bars (blue/red) to identify variances.

3.2 Viewing Baseline Data in Tables

1. Add baseline columns to the task table:
   - Right-click a column header, select **Insert Column**, and choose fields such as **Baseline Start**, **Baseline Finish**, or **Baseline Cost**.
2. Compare these fields with actual data fields like **Actual Start**, **Actual Finish**, or **Actual Cost**.

3.3 Using Variance Table

1. Switch to the **Variance Table**:
   - Go to **View > Tables > Variance**.
2. Review fields such as **Start Variance** and **Finish Variance** to identify schedule deviations.

---

4. Analyzing Key Metrics

4.1 Schedule Variance

- **Start Variance**: Difference between baseline start and actual start.
- **Finish Variance**: Difference between baseline finish and actual finish.

4.2 Cost Variance

- Compare **Baseline Cost** with **Actual Cost** to track budget performance.
- Identify over-budget tasks or resources.

4.3 Work Variance

- Analyze differences between **Baseline Work** and **Actual Work** to monitor resource usage.

---

5. Using Reports for Baseline vs. Actual Analysis

5.1 Built-In Reports

1. Navigate to **Report > Project Overview** or **Cost Overview**.
2. These reports provide visual summaries of baseline vs. actual performance.

5.2 Custom Reports

1. Go to **Report > New Report > Table Report**.
2. Include fields such as **Baseline Start**, **Baseline Cost**, **Actual Start**, and **Actual Cost**.
3. Use charts or tables to highlight variances.

---

6. Visualizing Performance Trends

6.1 Use Progress Lines

1. Go to **Format > Gridlines**.
2. Select **Progress Lines** to visualize task completion compared to the baseline.

6.2 Apply Conditional Formatting

- Highlight tasks with significant variances using custom filters or conditional formatting.

6.3 Use the Timeline View

- Add tasks to the timeline and overlay baseline and actual data for a high-level view of performance trends.

---

7. Tips for Effective Baseline vs. Actual Analysis

1. **Set Baselines Early**: Establish baselines as soon as the project plan is finalized.
2. **Monitor Regularly**: Review baseline vs. actual performance weekly to identify issues early.
3. **Focus on Critical Tasks**: Prioritize analyzing tasks on the critical path to avoid project delays.
4. **Document Changes**: Record reasons for variances to improve future project planning.
5. **Communicate Findings**: Share variance reports with stakeholders to ensure transparency.

---

8. Troubleshooting Common Issues

Problem: No Baseline Data Found

- **Solution**: Verify that a baseline has been set. Go to **Project > Set Baseline** to confirm.

Problem: Variance Data Seems Incorrect

- **Solution**: Check for tasks with manual scheduling or constraints that override baseline values.

Problem: Baseline Bars Not Displayed on Gantt Chart

- **Solution**: Enable baseline bars in **Format > Bar Styles**.

---

9. Summary

Reviewing baseline vs. actual performance is a crucial practice for ensuring project success. By leveraging Microsoft Project's tools to analyze variances, you can gain valuable insights into project trends, identify potential risks, and take corrective actions to keep the project on track.

Key Takeaways

- Set baselines to create a reference point for project performance.
- Use tools like the **Tracking Gantt View**, **Variance Table**, and reports to compare baseline vs. actual data.
- Focus on key metrics such as schedule variance, cost variance, and work variance.
- Regularly monitor performance and communicate findings with stakeholders.

In the next section, we'll explore working with views and tables, enabling you to customize and organize project data for better analysis and reporting.

Section VII:
Working with Views and Tables

Overview of Built-In Views

Microsoft Project offers a range of built-in views to help project managers visualize and analyze their project data. Each view is tailored to a specific aspect of project management, such as task schedules, resource allocation, or cost tracking. This chapter provides an overview of the built-in views, their purposes, and how to use them effectively.

1. What Are Built-In Views?

Built-in views in Microsoft Project are pre-configured layouts that present project data in various formats, such as tables, charts, and graphs. These views allow you to analyze tasks, resources, and progress from different perspectives.

1.1 Why Use Built-In Views?

- **Enhanced Visualization**: Gain a better understanding of project components.
- **Streamlined Analysis**: Access data relevant to specific project aspects.
- **Ease of Navigation**: Quickly switch between views to address different project needs.

2. Categories of Built-In Views

Microsoft Project organizes its views into task-based, resource-based, and combined categories.

2.1 Task-Based Views

- Focus on tasks, their dependencies, durations, and progress.
- Examples include:
    - **Gantt Chart**: Displays tasks as horizontal bars on a timeline.
    - **Task Sheet**: Provides a tabular view of task details.
    - **Calendar**: Presents tasks in a calendar format.

2.2 Resource-Based Views

- Highlight resource allocation, workload, and availability.
- Examples include:
    - **Resource Sheet**: Lists all resources and their attributes.
    - **Resource Usage**: Displays resource assignments and workloads over time.
    - **Team Planner**: Offers a drag-and-drop interface for managing resource tasks.

2.3 Combined Views

- Provide a holistic view of tasks and resources.
- Examples include:
    - **Timeline View**: Offers a high-level overview of project milestones and key tasks.

     ○ **Task Usage**: Combines task details with resource assignments.

---

3. Accessing and Switching Between Views

3.1 Using the View Tab

1. Navigate to the **View** tab on the Ribbon.
2. Select a view from the **Task Views** or **Resource Views** group.

3.2 View Bar

- The **View Bar** on the left side of the workspace provides quick access to common views.
- To enable the View Bar, go to **View > View Bar**.

3.3 Using the View Selector

- Click the view name in the bottom-left corner of the Microsoft Project window to open the **View Selector**.

---

4. Key Built-In Views

4.1 Gantt Chart View

- **Purpose**: Visualize task schedules and progress on a timeline.
- **Usage**:
  - ○ Use the task table to update task details.
  - ○ Track progress with bars that reflect task completion.

4.2 Resource Sheet View

- **Purpose**: Manage resource details, such as names, types, and availability.
- **Usage**:
  - ○ Add new resources or update resource attributes.
  - ○ Monitor resource max units to avoid overallocation.

4.3 Tracking Gantt View

- **Purpose**: Compare actual progress with the baseline schedule.
- **Usage**:
  - ○ View baseline bars alongside actual progress bars.
  - ○ Identify schedule variances visually.

4.4 Calendar View

- **Purpose**: Display tasks in a familiar calendar format.
- **Usage**:
  - ○ Highlight task deadlines and overlapping activities.
  - ○ Adjust task dates directly on the calendar.

4.5 Resource Usage View

- **Purpose**: Analyze resource workloads and assignments over time.
- **Usage**:
  - ○ Identify overallocations and redistribute work.

    ○ Add time-phased data columns like **Actual Work** and **Remaining Work**.

4.6 Timeline View

- **Purpose**: Provide a high-level overview of the project's key milestones and tasks.
- **Usage**:
  - ○ Add tasks to the timeline for visibility.
  - ○ Use for presentations or stakeholder updates.

4.7 Task Usage View

- **Purpose**: Combine task details with resource assignments.
- **Usage**:
  - ○ Review how resources contribute to individual tasks.
  - ○ Update work values directly in the grid.

---

5. Customizing Built-In Views

5.1 Adding Columns

- Right-click a column header and select **Insert Column**.
- Choose fields like **% Complete**, **Start Date**, or **Cost**.

5.2 Changing Timescales

- Right-click the timescale bar and adjust the time units (e.g., Days, Weeks, Months).

5.3 Filtering Data

- Apply filters to focus on specific tasks or resources:
  - ○ Go to **View > Filter** and select a predefined filter or create a custom one.

---

6. Tips for Using Built-In Views

1. **Choose the Right View**: Select views based on your analysis needs (e.g., use the Gantt Chart for scheduling and the Resource Usage view for workload analysis).
2. **Combine Views**: Use split views to display two views simultaneously for better insights.
3. **Customize Layouts**: Modify columns, timescales, and formatting to suit your project requirements.
4. **Save Frequently Used Views**: Save customized views for quick access in future sessions.
5. **Use Reports for Summary**: Complement detailed views with reports for stakeholder communication.

---

7. Troubleshooting Common Issues

Problem: Cannot Find a Specific View

- **Solution**: Ensure the view is enabled under **View > More Views**.

Problem: Data in the View Seems Incorrect

- **Solution**: Verify that all tasks and resources are updated with accurate data.

Problem: View Is Cluttered or Difficult to Read

- **Solution**: Filter or group data to simplify the display.

---

8. Summary

Built-in views in Microsoft Project are essential for managing tasks, resources, and schedules effectively. By understanding the purpose of each view and customizing them to meet your needs, you can enhance your ability to track progress, manage resources, and communicate updates to stakeholders.

Key Takeaways

- Use task-based views like **Gantt Chart** and **Tracking Gantt** for scheduling.
- Leverage resource-based views like **Resource Sheet** and **Resource Usage** for workload management.
- Customize views with filters, columns, and formatting to improve usability.
- Save custom layouts for future use and combine views for comprehensive analysis.

In the next chapter, we'll explore creating custom views and tables to tailor Microsoft Project further to your unique project management needs.

Creating Custom Views and Tables

While Microsoft Project provides an array of built-in views and tables, customizing these tools allows you to tailor the software to meet your specific project management needs. Custom views and tables enable you to focus on key metrics, streamline workflows, and enhance data presentation. This chapter explores how to create, modify, and effectively use custom views and tables.

---

1. Why Create Custom Views and Tables?

Customizing views and tables can:

- Highlight specific project details relevant to your goals.
- Improve team collaboration by focusing on shared priorities.
- Simplify reporting and stakeholder communication.

Examples of use cases include creating views for tracking overdue tasks, monitoring resource allocation, or analyzing project costs.

---

2. Creating Custom Views

2.1 Understanding Views in Microsoft Project

- Views are visual layouts that combine tables, charts, and graphical elements to present project data.
- Each view can be tailored to display specific fields, filters, and formats.

2.2 Steps to Create a Custom View

1. **Navigate to the View Tab**:
   - Go to **View > More Views**.
2. **Select New View**:
   - Click **New** to create a custom view.
3. **Choose a View Type**:
   - Select from options such as **Gantt Chart**, **Sheet**, **Usage**, or **Graphical**.
4. **Name Your View**:
   - Assign a meaningful name (e.g., "Overdue Tasks Tracker").
5. **Customize View Settings**:
   - Adjust table, filter, and group settings to focus on relevant data.
6. **Save the View**:
   - Click **OK** to save and make it available in the view list.

---

3. Customizing Tables in Microsoft Project

3.1 Understanding Tables

- Tables are the structured columns within a view, displaying data fields like task names, start dates, and percent complete.
- Customizing tables allows you to show, hide, or reorder fields for better analysis.

3.2 Steps to Create a Custom Table

1. **Open the Tables Menu**:
   - Navigate to **View > Tables > More Tables**.
2. **Select New Table**:
   - Click **New** to start creating a custom table.
3. **Define Table Columns**:
   - Add, remove, or rearrange columns.
   - For each column, specify the field (e.g., Task Name, Duration) and alignment.
4. **Set Column Widths**:
   - Adjust column widths to improve readability.
5. **Apply Formatting**:
   - Use bold or italics for key columns to emphasize important data.
6. **Save the Table**:
   - Name your table and click **OK** to save it for future use.

---

4. Combining Custom Views and Tables

Once you've created custom views and tables, you can combine them to create powerful analytical tools:

1. Open your custom view.
2. Assign your custom table to the view:
   - Go to **View > Tables > [Your Custom Table]**.
3. Save the combined setup for consistent use.

---

5. Applying Filters, Groups, and Sorting

5.1 Adding Filters

1. Create a filter to show specific data (e.g., tasks overdue by 7 days):
   - Go to **View > Filter > New Filter**.
2. Define criteria for the filter.
3. Apply the filter to your custom view or table.

5.2 Grouping Data

- Group data by categories like resource type, task priority, or project phase:
  - Go to **View > Group by > New Group**.
  - Customize group headers and sorting orders.

5.3 Sorting Data

- Sort data by fields like start date, cost, or task duration:
  - Right-click a column header and choose **Sort Ascending** or **Sort Descending**.

---

6. Formatting Custom Views

6.1 Formatting Gantt Charts

- Customize Gantt bars to reflect task types or statuses:
  - Go to **Format > Bar Styles**.
  - Assign unique colors or patterns to different task categories.

6.2 Highlighting Key Data

- Use conditional formatting to emphasize critical fields:
  - Apply filters or formatting rules to fields like cost overruns or delayed tasks.

---

7. Best Practices for Creating Custom Views and Tables

1. **Keep It Simple**: Avoid clutter by limiting columns and fields to essential data.
2. **Test and Refine**: Review your customizations to ensure they meet project needs.
3. **Save Frequently**: Save your customizations regularly to avoid losing changes.
4. **Use Naming Conventions**: Name views and tables clearly for easy identification.
5. **Share with Teams**: Export and share custom views and tables to improve collaboration.

---

8. Troubleshooting Common Issues

Problem: Custom View Not Displaying Correctly

- **Solution**: Verify that the correct table, filter, and grouping options are applied.

Problem: Data Missing in Custom Table

- **Solution**: Check if hidden fields or filters are excluding the data.

Problem: Customization Lost After Restart

- **Solution**: Save the project file and ensure custom views/tables are saved within it.

---

9. Summary

Custom views and tables are invaluable tools for tailoring Microsoft Project to suit specific project requirements. By creating and combining these elements, you can streamline workflows, enhance data analysis, and present information effectively to stakeholders.

Key Takeaways

- Use custom views to visualize data in a way that aligns with project goals.
- Design custom tables to display only the fields you need for analysis.
- Combine views, tables, filters, and groups for a comprehensive approach.
- Regularly save and share your customizations to ensure consistency across teams.

In the next chapter, we'll explore filtering and grouping data to further enhance your ability to focus on the most critical project details.

Filtering and Grouping Data

Microsoft Project's filtering and grouping features provide powerful ways to manage and analyze project data. Filtering allows you to focus on specific tasks or resources, while grouping organizes data based on shared attributes. This chapter explores how to effectively use these tools to streamline workflows and gain deeper insights into your project.

1. Overview of Filtering and Grouping

1.1 What Is Filtering?

Filtering displays only the data that meets specified criteria, hiding irrelevant information to help you focus.

- Example: Viewing only tasks that are overdue or resources that are overallocated.

1.2 What Is Grouping?

Grouping organizes data into categories based on shared attributes, making it easier to analyze trends or patterns.

- Example: Grouping tasks by priority or resources by department.

2. Using Filters in Microsoft Project

2.1 Applying Built-In Filters

1. Go to **View > Filter**.
2. Choose from predefined filters such as **Critical Tasks**, **Milestones**, or **Tasks with Deadlines**.

2.2 Creating Custom Filters

1. Navigate to **View > Filter > New Filter**.
2. Enter a name for your filter.
3. Define criteria by selecting fields, conditions, and values.
   - Example: Show tasks with a **% Complete** less than 50%.
4. Save the filter and apply it to your view.

2.3 Combining Filters

- Combine multiple criteria using **AND** or **OR** logic to refine your filters further.
- Example: Display tasks that are both **Critical** AND have a **Finish Date** within 7 days.

2.4 Clearing Filters

- To return to the full dataset, select **View > Filter > No Filter**.

3. Using Groups in Microsoft Project

3.1 Applying Built-In Groups

1. Go to **View > Group by**.
2. Select predefined groups like **Resource Type**, **Task Duration**, or **Cost Status**.

    ○   Example: Use **Resource Group** to view resource allocation by team or department.

3.2 Creating Custom Groups

1. Navigate to **View > Group by > More Groups > New**.
2. Enter a name for your group.
3. Choose the field you want to group by (e.g., **Priority**, **Task Owner**).
4. Define sorting order (Ascending or Descending).
5. Save the group and apply it to your view.

3.3 Nested Grouping

- Add multiple levels of grouping to organize data hierarchically.
- Example: Group tasks first by **Phase** and then by **Task Priority**.

---

4. Combining Filters and Groups

You can use filters and groups together for more targeted analysis.

1. Apply a filter to focus on specific data.
2. Add a group to organize the filtered data into meaningful categories.
   - Example: Filter tasks by **Overdue Status** and group them by **Assigned Resource**.

---

5. Practical Applications of Filtering and Grouping

5.1 Tracking Task Progress

- **Filter**: Use a filter to display tasks with **% Complete < 50%**.
- **Group**: Group the filtered tasks by **Assigned Resource** to see who is responsible.

5.2 Managing Resource Overallocations

- **Filter**: Apply the **Overallocated Resources** filter.
- **Group**: Group by **Resource Type** to identify overallocation trends by department.

5.3 Analyzing Costs

- **Filter**: Show tasks with **Cost > $10,000**.
- **Group**: Group by **Cost Status** to separate over-budget and on-budget tasks.

---

6. Customizing Filtered and Grouped Views

6.1 Adding Columns

- Add relevant fields to your view for more detailed analysis.
- Example: Add the **Deadline** column when filtering for overdue tasks.

6.2 Highlighting Key Data

- Use conditional formatting or colored bars to emphasize critical tasks or milestones.

6.3 Saving Custom Views

- Save your filtered and grouped configurations as a new view for quick access:
  - Go to **View > More Views > New View** and include your filter and group settings.

---

7. Tips for Effective Filtering and Grouping

1. **Start with Built-In Options**: Use predefined filters and groups as a starting point before creating custom configurations.
2. **Combine Filters and Groups**: Leverage both tools together to maximize clarity and insights.
3. **Use Meaningful Names**: Clearly name custom filters and groups for easy identification.
4. **Save Frequently Used Configurations**: Save your customizations as views for consistent use.
5. **Test for Accuracy**: Verify that your filters and groups display the intended data.

---

8. Troubleshooting Common Issues

Problem: Filter Returns No Data

- **Solution**: Double-check your criteria for accuracy. Ensure the data you're filtering exists in the project.

Problem: Grouping Is Incorrect

- **Solution**: Verify that the field you selected for grouping has valid data.

Problem: Filter or Group Not Applying to a View

- **Solution**: Confirm that the active view supports filters or groups (e.g., Task Views vs. Resource Views).

---

9. Summary

Filtering and grouping are essential tools for managing complex projects in Microsoft Project. They enable you to focus on specific aspects of your project, analyze data effectively, and present information clearly to stakeholders.

Key Takeaways

- Use filters to narrow down data and groups to categorize it meaningfully.
- Combine filters and groups for advanced analysis.
- Save custom configurations as views for future use.
- Regularly update filters and groups to reflect project changes.

In the next chapter, we'll delve into customizing Gantt chart elements to further enhance project visualization.

Customizing Gantt Chart Elements

The Gantt chart is one of the most powerful tools in Microsoft Project, providing a visual representation of task schedules, dependencies, and progress. Customizing its elements can significantly enhance its utility by tailoring it to your specific project needs. This chapter covers the techniques to modify and enhance Gantt chart elements for better visualization and communication.

1. Why Customize Gantt Chart Elements?

Customizing the Gantt chart allows you to:

- Highlight critical tasks and milestones.
- Enhance clarity for team members and stakeholders.
- Focus on specific aspects of the project, such as resource allocation or task constraints.

2. Accessing Gantt Chart Customization Tools

To customize Gantt chart elements, use the **Format** tab on the Ribbon. This tab becomes active when the Gantt chart is selected.

3. Customizing Task Bars

3.1 Changing Bar Colors and Styles

1. Go to **Format > Bar Styles**.
2. Select a task category (e.g., Critical, Milestone, Summary).
3. Adjust the following:
   - **Color**: Choose a distinct color for easy identification.
   - **Shape**: Modify the bar shape (e.g., solid, dashed).
   - **Pattern**: Apply patterns for additional differentiation.
4. Click **OK** to apply changes.

3.2 Adding Text to Bars

1. Open **Format > Bar Styles**.
2. In the **Text** column, select where to place text (e.g., Left, Right, Top, Bottom).
3. Choose a field to display (e.g., Task Name, Start Date).

3.3 Highlighting Critical Tasks

- Enable the **Critical Tasks** option in **Format > Bar Styles** to automatically highlight tasks on the critical path.

4. Modifying Gridlines

Gridlines can help structure your Gantt chart for better readability.

4.1 Customizing Gridline Styles

1. Go to **Format > Gridlines**.
2. Select a gridline type (e.g., Current Date, Project Start, Project Finish).
3. Choose a line style, color, and width.
4. Click **OK** to save changes.

4.2 Adding Progress Lines

Progress lines show the deviation between planned and actual progress.

1. Navigate to **Format > Progress Lines**.
2. Adjust settings to display lines at specific intervals or dates.

---

5. Adjusting Timescales

The timescale determines how the timeline is displayed at the top of the Gantt chart.

5.1 Changing Timescale Units

1. Right-click the timescale area.
2. Select **Timescale** to adjust the units (e.g., Days, Weeks, Months).

5.2 Adding Additional Timescale Tiers

- Display up to three tiers (e.g., Quarter, Month, Week):
  1. Open **Timescale Settings**.
  2. Configure each tier's format and label style.

---

6. Using Conditional Formatting

Conditional formatting can highlight tasks that meet specific criteria, such as overdue tasks or those with high priority.

1. Go to **View > Gantt Chart > Customize Colors and Styles**.
2. Apply conditional rules based on task attributes.
3. For example, set overdue tasks to display in red.

---

7. Creating and Applying Custom Gantt Chart Views

Save your customizations as a unique view to reuse them later.

7.1 Creating a Custom View

1. Go to **View > More Views > New View**.
2. Select **Gantt Chart** as the view type.
3. Name your view and apply your customizations.

7.2 Applying the Custom View

1. Go to **View > More Views**.
2. Select your custom view and click **Apply**.

---

8. Adding Annotations and Visual Indicators

Annotations and indicators provide additional context to your Gantt chart.

8.1 Using Text Boxes

- Add text boxes for comments or additional information:
    1. Go to **Format > Drawing > Text Box**.
    2. Place the text box on the Gantt chart and type your annotation.

8.2 Applying Graphical Indicators

- Use graphical indicators to represent task statuses visually:
    1. Customize the field with conditional formatting (e.g., red flag for overdue tasks).

---

9. Sharing Customized Gantt Charts

9.1 Exporting as an Image or PDF

1. Go to **File > Export**.
2. Select a format (e.g., PDF or PNG).

9.2 Printing the Gantt Chart

1. Go to **File > Print**.
2. Adjust page settings to include all relevant data.

---

10. Tips for Effective Customization

1. **Keep It Simple**: Avoid overloading the chart with too many details or colors.
2. **Focus on Key Elements**: Highlight critical tasks, milestones, and dependencies.
3. **Use Consistent Styles**: Ensure consistent formatting across all Gantt charts in the project.
4. **Test Your Customizations**: Preview your changes to confirm they improve readability and clarity.

---

11. Troubleshooting Common Issues

Problem: Customizations Not Visible

- **Solution**: Ensure the active view is the Gantt chart.

Problem: Bars Overlap or Misalign

- **Solution**: Adjust the task bar spacing in **Format > Layout**.

Problem: Timescale Too Cluttered

- **Solution**: Use higher-level units (e.g., weeks or months) for larger projects.

---

12. Summary

Customizing Gantt chart elements transforms Microsoft Project from a planning tool into a powerful communication medium. By tailoring task bars, gridlines, timescales, and annotations, you can create clear, visually appealing Gantt charts that effectively convey project information.

Key Takeaways

- Use the **Format** tab to customize task bars, gridlines, and timescales.
- Highlight critical tasks and milestones with distinctive styles.
- Save customizations as unique views for consistent application.
- Leverage annotations and indicators to enhance clarity.

In the next section, we'll explore reporting and visualizations to further enhance how you communicate project progress and performance.

Section VIII:
Reporting and Visualizations

Generating Standard Reports

Microsoft Project provides a suite of standard reports that enable project managers to communicate project performance, progress, and key metrics effectively. These reports are pre-designed and require minimal customization, making them a great starting point for presenting project data. In this chapter, you'll learn how to access, use, and customize standard reports to meet your reporting needs.

1. Overview of Standard Reports

Standard reports in Microsoft Project cover a wide range of project management topics, including:

- **Project Overview**: Summarizes key project details and progress.
- **Resource Reports**: Focus on resource allocation, availability, and workload.
- **Task Reports**: Highlight task statuses, progress, and critical tasks.
- **Cost Reports**: Provide insights into budget performance and expenditures.

These reports are pre-formatted and ready to use, requiring only project data input.

2. Accessing Standard Reports

2.1 Navigating to Reports

1. Go to the **Report** tab on the Ribbon.
2. Click **Reports** to open the **Report Gallery**.
3. Choose a report category:
   - **Dashboards**
   - **Resources**
   - **Costs**
   - **In Progress**

2.2 Previewing a Report

- Select a report from the gallery to preview it in the main workspace.
- Use the zoom and scroll options to review the report layout and content.

3. Types of Standard Reports

3.1 Dashboard Reports

These provide a high-level overview of project health and progress.

- **Project Overview**: Displays project name, status, and key dates.
- **Work Overview**: Summarizes total work, completed work, and remaining work.
- **Cost Overview**: Highlights budget, actual costs, and remaining costs.

3.2 Resource Reports

These focus on resource allocation and utilization.

- **Resource Overview**: Provides a snapshot of resource availability and assignments.
- **Overallocated Resources**: Identifies resources with excessive workloads.
- **Cost per Resource**: Breaks down costs by resource.

3.3 Cost Reports

These track budget performance and financial health.

- **Cash Flow**: Shows cost distribution over time.
- **Budget Overview**: Compares planned and actual costs.
- **Earned Value**: Provides earned value metrics for performance evaluation.

3.4 Task Reports

These detail task progress and performance.

- **Critical Tasks**: Highlights tasks on the critical path.
- **Slipping Tasks**: Identifies tasks with delays.
- **Milestones**: Summarizes key milestones and their statuses.

---

4. Customizing Standard Reports

While standard reports are pre-designed, you can customize them to suit your needs.

4.1 Adding Fields and Data

1. Open a report and click **Design > Report Tools**.
2. Select **Insert > Chart, Table, or Text Box** to add new elements.
3. Choose the fields to display, such as **Task Name**, **Start Date**, or **Actual Cost**.

4.2 Changing Chart Types

1. Click on a chart within the report.
2. Go to **Design > Chart Tools > Change Chart Type**.
3. Select a new chart type (e.g., bar chart, pie chart).

4.3 Adjusting Layout and Formatting

- Resize or reposition elements using drag-and-drop.
- Modify fonts, colors, and borders via the **Format** tab.

4.4 Applying Filters and Sorting

1. Click on a table or chart.
2. Use the **Field List** pane to apply filters (e.g., show only critical tasks).
3. Sort data by attributes like start date or cost.

---

5. Exporting and Sharing Reports

5.1 Exporting to PDF or Image Format

1. Go to **File > Export**.
2. Choose **PDF** or **Image** as the export format.
3. Save the report to your desired location.

5.2 Printing Reports

1. Go to **File > Print**.
2. Adjust print settings, including orientation and scaling.
3. Preview the report before printing.

5.3 Sharing via Email or Cloud

- Save the report as a PDF and share it via email or cloud storage.
- Export the data to Excel for additional formatting before sharing.

---

6. Best Practices for Using Standard Reports

1. **Understand Your Audience**: Tailor the report to the needs of stakeholders, focusing on metrics they care about.
2. **Review Data Accuracy**: Ensure project data is up-to-date before generating reports.
3. **Leverage Filters**: Use filters to focus on specific tasks, resources, or timeframes.
4. **Combine Reports**: Use multiple reports to provide a comprehensive view of project performance.
5. **Document Customizations**: Keep track of any changes made to standard reports for future use.

---

7. Troubleshooting Common Issues

Problem: Report Shows Incomplete Data

- **Solution**: Check that all relevant fields are populated in the project file.

Problem: Charts or Tables Are Misaligned

- **Solution**: Adjust layout and formatting using the **Design** tab.

Problem: Report Does Not Meet Stakeholder Needs

- **Solution**: Customize the report or combine it with other reports to provide the necessary details.

8. Summary

Standard reports in Microsoft Project offer a quick and effective way to communicate project information. By understanding the available options and customizing them as needed, you can ensure your reports provide meaningful insights to stakeholders.

Key Takeaways

- Use dashboard reports for high-level summaries.
- Resource and cost reports are essential for monitoring budget and workload.
- Task reports provide detailed insights into progress and schedules.
- Customize standard reports to align with project-specific requirements.

In the next chapter, we'll explore how to create custom reports and dashboards for even greater flexibility and control over your project reporting.

Creating Custom Reports and Dashboards

Custom reports and dashboards provide you with a unique way to present your project data, allowing for flexibility in how information is displayed and communicated. This chapter will guide you through the process of creating custom reports and dashboards, enabling you to tailor your project's reporting to meet specific stakeholder needs and project requirements.

1. Overview of Custom Reports and Dashboards

1.1 What Is a Custom Report?

A custom report in Microsoft Project allows you to design a report that specifically meets your needs. Unlike standard reports, which are pre-designed, custom reports can include the exact fields, data, and layouts that you want to present to stakeholders.

1.2 What Is a Dashboard?

A dashboard is a high-level report that aggregates key project metrics into an easy-to-read format. It can be composed of various charts, tables, and graphical elements, offering a snapshot of the project's health at a glance.

2. Creating Custom Reports

2.1 Accessing the Report Designer

To create a custom report, you need to access the **Report Designer**:

1. Navigate to the **Report** tab on the Ribbon.
2. Click **New Report** under the **Report Gallery** group.
3. Select **Blank** to create a report from scratch, or choose an existing template to modify.

2.2 Choosing the Report Type

Once in the **Report Designer**, you'll choose the type of report you want to create:

- **Chart**: Use charts to visually represent data.
- **Table**: Use tables for detailed data presentation.
- **Text**: Use text boxes for additional notes or explanations.

2.3 Adding Data to Your Custom Report

1. Go to **Design** in the **Report Tools** tab.
2. Choose **Insert** to add elements such as:
   - **Tables** (e.g., task lists, resource assignments).
   - **Charts** (e.g., Gantt charts, pie charts, bar charts).
   - **Text Boxes** for custom annotations.
3. Choose fields to display in your report by selecting from the **Field List** pane. You can add data such as **Task Name**, **Start Date**, **% Complete**, and **Cost**.
4. Customize how the data is presented—change text size, color, and format for better readability.

2.4 Customizing Layout and Formatting

1. Adjust the layout by moving report elements around. You can resize, reposition, and format each component (e.g., tables, charts) using drag-and-drop or alignment tools.
2. Format your report to match your project's branding or specific requirements (e.g., adjusting colors, fonts, and borders).

2.5 Saving Your Custom Report

1. Once your report is designed, save it by selecting **File > Save As**.
2. Name the report and choose where to save it for easy access later.

---

3. Creating Custom Dashboards

3.1 Why Use Dashboards?

Dashboards are ideal for summarizing project status, performance, and key metrics at a glance. Custom dashboards allow you to integrate various data points and visual elements, providing stakeholders with a snapshot of the project's overall health and progress.

3.2 Starting a New Dashboard

1. Navigate to **Report > New Report**.
2. Choose **Dashboard** as the report type.
3. Select **Blank Dashboard** or use a template to get started.

3.3 Adding Elements to a Dashboard

Dashboards can include multiple elements such as:

- **Charts** (e.g., bar, pie, line) to visualize progress.
- **Tables** to list detailed information (e.g., task names, due dates).
- **Text Boxes** for annotations or high-level comments.
- **Indicators** for highlighting key metrics such as cost variances, task completion rates, or resource utilization.
1. In the **Design** tab, click **Insert** to add the necessary elements (chart, table, etc.).
2. Choose the data you want to display in each element. For instance, you might use a pie chart to represent the distribution of task completion percentages.
3. Customize the appearance of your dashboard elements. You can change chart types, add colors, and format tables to make the data clearer.

3.4 Organizing Your Dashboard Layout

- Arrange the dashboard elements in a logical order, focusing on the most important information first.
- Use grids to align items neatly, ensuring the dashboard is aesthetically pleasing and easy to read.
- Add titles or section headers to clarify what each element represents (e.g., **Project Status**, **Resource Allocation**).

3.5 Customizing Data in Dashboards

Use the **Field List** to select which data fields you want to display. For example, you might want to add:

- **Task Status** (Not Started, In Progress, Completed).
- **Cost vs. Budget** for financial performance.
- **Workload Allocation** for resource management.

You can filter and sort the data within each element to display specific subsets of the project data.

3.6 Saving and Sharing Dashboards

1. Save your custom dashboard by selecting **File > Save As** and giving it a meaningful name.
2. Dashboards can be exported to other formats, like PDF or image files, for sharing with stakeholders.

---

4. Best Practices for Creating Custom Reports and Dashboards

1. **Know Your Audience**: Tailor the content and format of reports and dashboards to the needs of your stakeholders. Focus on the metrics that matter most to them.
2. **Keep It Simple**: Avoid clutter by focusing on key data. Dashboards should be clear and concise, highlighting project health and critical issues.
3. **Ensure Data Accuracy**: Ensure that your reports and dashboards reflect the most up-to-date and accurate project data.
4. **Use Visuals Wisely**: Leverage charts and graphs to help communicate complex data quickly and clearly.
5. **Save and Reuse**: Once you've created a custom report or dashboard, save it for future use and share it with your team. This will save you time and ensure consistency across reports.

---

5. Troubleshooting Common Issues

Problem: Data Does Not Appear in Reports or Dashboards

- **Solution**: Verify that the correct fields have been selected and that the data is present in the project file. Double-check your data entry for completeness.

Problem: Elements Overlap in Dashboards

- **Solution**: Adjust the layout by resizing or repositioning elements to fit neatly within the page. Ensure there's enough space between elements.

Problem: Report Formatting Is Inconsistent

- **Solution**: Ensure you are using consistent fonts, colors, and styles across all elements. Use the **Format** tab to adjust the appearance of each element to match the rest of the report.

---

6. Summary

Creating custom reports and dashboards in Microsoft Project allows you to communicate project status and progress in a tailored, visually impactful way. By customizing the data, layout, and design, you can ensure your reports and dashboards meet the specific needs of your stakeholders.

Key Takeaways

- Use custom reports to focus on the most relevant project data for your stakeholders.
- Dashboards provide a high-level view of project health and performance.
- Save and reuse custom reports and dashboards for future projects.
- Apply best practices for clarity, simplicity, and accuracy in reporting.

In the next chapter, we will explore how to utilize charts and graphical indicators to enhance your project visualizations even further.

Utilizing Charts and Graphical Indicators

Charts and graphical indicators in Microsoft Project offer a powerful way to visualize project data, enabling stakeholders to quickly grasp progress, resource usage, cost performance, and other key metrics. This chapter explores the different types of charts and graphical indicators available in Microsoft Project and how to use them effectively to enhance reporting and decision-making.

1. Importance of Visualizing Project Data

1.1 Why Use Charts and Graphical Indicators?

Visual representations of data are often more effective than textual or numerical formats for:

- Highlighting trends and patterns.
- Comparing planned vs. actual performance.
- Communicating complex information quickly to diverse audiences.

1.2 Benefits of Visual Elements in Reports

- Simplify communication with stakeholders who may not be familiar with technical project details.
- Make it easier to identify bottlenecks, risks, or areas requiring immediate attention.
- Provide a clear summary of progress for executives and team members.

2. Types of Charts in Microsoft Project

Microsoft Project offers several types of charts to display data effectively.

2.1 Gantt Charts

- **Description**: Displays tasks along a timeline, showing start and end dates, dependencies, and progress.
- **Usage**: Ideal for visualizing the overall schedule and task relationships.
- **Customization**:
    - Change bar colors to represent task categories (e.g., critical tasks, milestones).
    - Add labels to bars for better clarity.

2.2 Bar and Column Charts

- **Description**: Use bars or columns to compare data such as resource allocation or task completion.
- **Usage**: Great for showing comparisons (e.g., planned vs. actual work, budget vs. actual cost).

2.3 Pie Charts

- **Description**: Visualizes proportions or percentages (e.g., task status, resource usage).
- **Usage**: Use pie charts to show how resources or costs are distributed across tasks or phases.

2.4 Line Charts

- **Description**: Tracks changes over time, such as cumulative progress or cost performance.
- **Usage**: Best for displaying trends (e.g., earned value analysis).

2.5 Combination Charts

- **Description**: Combine multiple chart types (e.g., line and bar) to represent complex relationships.
- **Usage**: Useful for correlating multiple data points (e.g., task progress vs. budget expenditure).

---

3. Using Graphical Indicators

Graphical indicators provide visual cues such as icons or color-coded symbols to highlight key metrics.

3.1 Built-In Graphical Indicators

- **Examples**:
  - **Green, Yellow, Red Lights**: Indicate task or project status (e.g., on track, at risk, delayed).
  - **Arrow Icons**: Show trends, such as cost increases or decreases.
  - **Checkmarks**: Represent completed tasks or milestones.

3.2 Applying Graphical Indicators

1. Go to the **Format** tab in the Ribbon.
2. Select a field or column (e.g., % Complete, Status).
3. Apply conditional formatting to display graphical indicators based on specific criteria.

3.3 Customizing Graphical Indicators

1. In the **Customize Fields** menu, select a field to add graphical indicators.
2. Define rules (e.g., "if % Complete = 100, show a green checkmark").
3. Test and adjust the rules to ensure they reflect accurate project conditions.

---

4. Adding Charts and Indicators to Reports

4.1 Creating a Chart

1. Navigate to the **Report** tab and select a report to customize.
2. Click **Design > Insert Chart** and choose a chart type.
3. Select the data fields to include in the chart (e.g., Start Date, Duration, Resource Names).

4.2 Integrating Graphical Indicators

1. Add a table or column to the report.
2. Apply graphical indicators to fields such as **Task Status** or **Cost Variance**.
3. Adjust the layout to ensure the indicators are visible and aligned.

4.3 Formatting Charts and Indicators

- Use the **Format** tab to adjust colors, fonts, and chart elements.
- Add legends or labels to make charts and indicators more intuitive.
- Align graphical indicators next to related data for easy interpretation.

---

5. Best Practices for Using Charts and Indicators

5.1 Match the Visualization to the Data

- Use Gantt charts for schedule tracking.
- Use bar charts for comparisons.

- Use pie charts for proportional data.

5.2 Keep It Simple

Avoid overloading charts with too much data. Focus on the key metrics that matter to your audience.

5.3 Use Consistent Formatting

- Apply consistent colors and styles across all charts and indicators to maintain clarity.
- Align visual elements with the project's branding guidelines if applicable.

5.4 Test the Accuracy of Data

Ensure the data feeding into charts and indicators is accurate and up-to-date before sharing with stakeholders.

5.5 Align with Stakeholder Needs

Tailor charts and graphical indicators to highlight the information most relevant to the stakeholders reviewing the report.

---

6. Troubleshooting Common Issues

Problem: Charts Are Not Displaying Data Correctly

- **Solution**: Verify that all fields are populated with accurate data in the project file.

Problem: Indicators Are Misaligned or Missing

- **Solution**: Check the conditional formatting rules and adjust as needed.

Problem: Chart Layout Is Crowded

- **Solution**: Simplify the chart by reducing the number of data points or splitting information into multiple charts.

---

7. Summary

Charts and graphical indicators are essential tools for presenting project data in a visually engaging and informative way. By understanding the available options and applying them strategically, you can enhance your reports and ensure stakeholders have a clear understanding of project performance.

Key Takeaways

- Use Gantt charts for schedule visualization and bar charts for comparisons.
- Leverage graphical indicators to highlight task and project statuses.
- Customize and format charts to align with project needs and stakeholder expectations.
- Test your visualizations to ensure accuracy and clarity.

In the next chapter, we will explore how to export reports and visualizations for sharing with team members and stakeholders.

Exporting Reports to Other Formats

Exporting reports to other formats is a critical step in sharing project information with stakeholders who may not have access to Microsoft Project or who prefer data in alternative formats. Microsoft Project provides various options to export reports, ensuring that your project data is both accessible and presentable.

1. Importance of Exporting Reports

Exporting reports enables project managers to:

- Share data with stakeholders in their preferred format (PDF, Excel, Word, etc.).
- Collaborate with external teams or clients who may not use Microsoft Project.
- Archive project reports for future reference or audits.

Exporting also ensures data portability, allowing integration with other software tools for analysis or reporting.

2. Formats Available for Export

Microsoft Project supports the following export formats:

1. **PDF**: Ideal for non-editable, professional-looking reports.
2. **Excel**: Used for detailed data analysis and customization.
3. **Word**: Suitable for creating text-rich, formatted documents.
4. **Image Files (e.g., PNG, JPEG)**: Useful for including visual data in presentations or documents.
5. **XML**: Enables integration with other project management tools.
6. **CSV**: Used for lightweight data sharing or import into spreadsheets.
7. **SharePoint or Online Platforms**: For collaborative sharing.

3. Exporting Reports as PDF

PDF is one of the most commonly used formats for sharing reports due to its professional appearance and ease of distribution.

Steps to Export as PDF

1. Open the desired report in Microsoft Project.
2. Go to **File > Save As**.
3. Choose the location to save the file.
4. Select **PDF** from the **Save as type** dropdown menu.
5. Click **Save**.

Tips for PDF Export

- Ensure the report layout is optimized for printing or digital viewing.
- Use the **Print Preview** feature to adjust margins and orientation.
- Include a table of contents or labels if the report is lengthy.

4. Exporting Reports to Excel

Exporting to Excel is useful for conducting advanced calculations, creating pivot tables, or integrating data with other tools.

Steps to Export as Excel File

1. Navigate to the report or data table you wish to export.
2. Click **File > Save As**.
3. Choose a save location and select **Excel Workbook (*.xlsx)** from the **Save as type** dropdown.
4. Use the **Export Wizard** to customize the data fields you want to include (e.g., tasks, resources, timelines).
5. Click **Finish** to generate the Excel file.

Excel Export Considerations

- Ensure data columns are properly labeled for easy navigation.
- Use Excel's built-in formatting tools to enhance readability.
- Double-check for any loss of data formatting during the export process.

---

5. Exporting Reports to Word

Exporting to Word is ideal for creating narrative reports with embedded visuals.

Steps to Export to Word

1. Generate the report in Microsoft Project.
2. Copy the report content by selecting the data or chart and pressing **Ctrl + C**.
3. Open Microsoft Word and paste the content using **Ctrl + V**.
4. Format the report to include headers, footers, and other textual elements.

Alternatively, use the **Save As** feature to directly save as a Word document.

Enhancements for Word Reports

- Include tables, charts, and graphical indicators.
- Add a summary or executive overview at the beginning of the report.
- Use Word styles to maintain consistency in formatting.

---

6. Exporting Reports as Image Files

Charts or graphical reports can be exported as images to use in presentations or external documents.

Steps to Export as an Image

1. Open the report and select the chart or visual you wish to export.
2. Right-click and choose **Copy**.
3. Paste the visual into an image editor or directly into a document.
4. Save the visual as an image file (e.g., PNG or JPEG).

Best Practices for Image Exports

- Use high-resolution settings for clarity.
- Test the image on different devices to ensure readability.

7. Exporting to XML and CSV

XML and CSV formats are often used for data interchange and integration with other software.

Exporting as XML

1. Go to **File > Save As**.
2. Select **XML Data (*.xml)** as the file format.
3. Save the file and ensure compatibility with the target system.

Exporting as CSV

1. Use the **Export Wizard** to define the data fields.
2. Save the file as **Comma-Separated Values (*.csv)**.
3. Open the CSV in a spreadsheet application to verify the data layout.

8. Exporting Reports to SharePoint or Online Platforms

If your organization uses SharePoint or Microsoft 365, exporting directly to these platforms simplifies collaboration.

Steps for SharePoint Export

1. Connect your Microsoft Project file to SharePoint by going to **File > Info > Manage Accounts**.
2. Select **Save to SharePoint** and choose the destination folder.
3. Export the report in your desired format and upload it to SharePoint.

Online Collaboration Tips

- Ensure proper permissions are set for viewing and editing the reports.
- Use real-time collaboration features to gather feedback from stakeholders.

9. Best Practices for Exporting Reports

9.1 Tailor Reports to the Audience

- Use PDFs for external stakeholders requiring polished, finalized reports.
- Provide Excel or CSV files for team members who need to manipulate the data.

9.2 Check for Formatting Issues

- Preview the report in the exported format to ensure accuracy.
- Resolve any alignment, layout, or data truncation issues.

9.3 Automate Regular Exports

- Use macros or templates to streamline the export process for recurring reports.

10. Troubleshooting Export Issues

Problem: Data Missing in Exported Report

- **Solution**: Verify that all fields are populated in the Microsoft Project file.

Problem: Charts Do Not Appear in Export

- **Solution**: Ensure all visuals are selected and included in the report layout.

Problem: Formatting Is Lost

- **Solution**: Use the **Export Wizard** to customize settings and avoid compatibility issues.

---

11. Summary

Exporting reports to other formats allows project managers to effectively communicate project progress, performance, and outcomes to various stakeholders. By selecting the right export format and following best practices, you can ensure your reports are both accessible and impactful.

Key Takeaways

- Use PDFs for professional, non-editable reports.
- Export to Excel or CSV for data analysis and manipulation.
- Optimize visuals and layouts for clarity in all exported formats.
- Align the export format with the needs of your audience.

Next Section: Collaboration and Integration!

Section IX:
Collaboration and Integration

Sharing Project Files

Sharing project files effectively is an essential skill for project managers working with Microsoft Project. It ensures seamless collaboration, maintains version control, and fosters transparent communication among stakeholders. In this chapter, we will explore various methods and best practices for sharing Microsoft Project files, tailoring them to diverse project environments.

1. Importance of Sharing Project Files

Project success often depends on effective collaboration. Sharing project files enables:

- **Collaboration**: Teams can access real-time updates, reducing miscommunication.
- **Accountability**: Stakeholders can track progress and responsibilities.
- **Transparency**: Provides a clear view of project scope, timelines, and resources.
- **Version Control**: Ensures all users work with the latest file version.

2. File Sharing Options in Microsoft Project

Microsoft Project supports multiple methods for sharing files, catering to both local and cloud-based collaboration.

2.1 Sharing via Email

- **When to Use**: Ideal for quick, one-time sharing with individuals.
- **Steps**:
    - Save your project file.
    - Attach the file to an email as a **.mpp**, **PDF**, or other supported format.
    - Add recipients and send.
- **Considerations**:
    - Ensure recipients have the required software to open the file.
    - Avoid frequent email exchanges to reduce version control issues.

2.2 Saving to Shared Network Drives

- **When to Use**: Suitable for internal teams with shared access to network drives.
- **Steps**:
    - Save the project file to a shared folder on your organization's network.
    - Grant appropriate access permissions to team members.
- **Considerations**:
    - Regularly update the shared file to prevent outdated versions.
    - Monitor access to maintain file security.

2.3 Using Microsoft OneDrive

- **When to Use**: Ideal for cloud-based sharing and integration with other Microsoft 365 tools.
- **Steps**:
    - Save the file to **OneDrive** from within Microsoft Project by selecting **File > Save As > OneDrive**.
    - Share the file link by selecting **Share** and entering the email addresses of collaborators.
- **Benefits**:
    - Real-time collaboration.
    - Access from multiple devices.
    - Automatic version history.

2.4 Sharing Through SharePoint

- **When to Use**: Best for organizations using Microsoft SharePoint for project management.
- **Steps**:
    - Save your file to a SharePoint library.
    - Set file permissions to control who can view or edit the project.
    - Share the link with team members.
- **Benefits**:
    - Centralized storage.
    - Integration with Microsoft Project Online for enhanced collaboration.

2.5 Exporting to Other Formats

- **When to Use**: Useful when recipients do not have Microsoft Project.
- **Formats Supported**:
    1. **PDF**: For non-editable sharing.
    2. **Excel**: For data analysis.
    3. **Word**: For narrative reports.
    4. **Image Formats**: For visuals such as Gantt charts.
- **Steps**:
    1. Export the project in the desired format (e.g., **File > Export**).
    2. Share via email, cloud storage, or physical media.

3. Collaborating in Real-Time

Real-time collaboration is a powerful way to keep all stakeholders aligned.

3.1 Using Microsoft Teams

- Microsoft Teams integrates seamlessly with Microsoft Project, enabling team communication and file sharing.
- **Steps**:
    1. Upload the project file to a Teams channel.
    2. Use the **Files** tab to manage and edit the file collaboratively.
    3. Discuss updates in real-time through the chat or video call features.

3.2 Co-Authoring with Project Online

- Project Online supports simultaneous edits by multiple users.
- **Steps**:
    1. Publish the project file to Project Online.
    2. Grant permissions to team members.
    3. Collaborate through the web interface or desktop client.

---

4. Best Practices for Sharing Project Files

4.1 Maintain Version Control

- Use a versioning system to track changes and prevent confusion.
- Example: Name files with version numbers (e.g., "Project_Plan_v1.0.mpp").

4.2 Use Password Protection

- Protect sensitive project data by encrypting files or using password protection.
- **Steps**:
    1. Go to **File > Info > Protect Document**.
    2. Set a password for file access.

4.3 Define Access Permissions

- Limit editing access to authorized users.
- Use tools like OneDrive or SharePoint to set permissions.

4.4 Communicate Changes

- Notify team members of significant updates or revisions.
- Use project management tools to share updates (e.g., Teams, Project Online).

---

5. Troubleshooting Common Sharing Issues

Issue 1: Recipients Cannot Open the File

- **Solution**: Confirm they have the necessary software. If not, export the file to a compatible format like PDF or Excel.

Issue 2: File Conflicts on Shared Drives

- **Solution**: Encourage team members to work on local copies and synchronize updates.

Issue 3: Real-Time Collaboration Lag

- **Solution**: Check internet connectivity and ensure all users have compatible software versions.

---

6. Summary

Sharing project files effectively ensures smooth collaboration, better communication, and improved project outcomes. Whether through email, cloud storage, or integrated tools like SharePoint and Teams, Microsoft Project provides a range of options to meet your team's needs.

Key Takeaways

- Choose the sharing method based on team requirements and available tools.
- Prioritize file security and version control.
- Leverage real-time collaboration tools for enhanced productivity.

In the next chapter, we will explore how to synchronize Microsoft Project with Microsoft 365 tools for an integrated project management experience.

Synchronizing with Microsoft 365 Tools

Microsoft Project integrates seamlessly with Microsoft 365 tools, enabling project managers to collaborate effectively, streamline workflows, and enhance productivity. Synchronizing Microsoft Project with Microsoft 365 applications like Teams, Outlook, and SharePoint ensures real-time collaboration and efficient resource management.

1. Why Synchronize Microsoft Project with Microsoft 365 Tools?

1.1 Enhanced Collaboration

- Real-time updates ensure team members and stakeholders work with the latest project data.
- Communication is streamlined through platforms like Microsoft Teams.

1.2 Improved Task and Resource Management

- Integration allows tasks and schedules to be synchronized with individual calendars in Outlook.
- Centralized resource management helps avoid conflicts and overallocations.

1.3 Efficient Document Sharing

- Share project documents and reports effortlessly using SharePoint and OneDrive.

1.4 Data Consolidation

- Integration consolidates project data with other organizational workflows, improving decision-making.

2. Key Microsoft 365 Tools for Integration

2.1 Microsoft Teams

- Enables chat, video conferencing, and file sharing.
- Provides a centralized location for project discussions.

2.2 SharePoint

- Offers a secure document repository.
- Allows version control and advanced file sharing.

2.3 Outlook

- Synchronizes project tasks with team members' calendars.
- Sends automatic reminders for deadlines and updates.

2.4 OneDrive

- Simplifies cloud storage and sharing for project files.
- Facilitates access from multiple devices.

2.5 Power BI

- Integrates for advanced data visualization and reporting.
- Creates dynamic dashboards for stakeholders.

3. Setting Up Microsoft Project Integration

3.1 Connecting to Microsoft Teams

1. Open Microsoft Project.
2. Navigate to **File > Info > Project Web App**.
3. Log in with your Microsoft 365 credentials.
4. Select the project file and choose **Sync with Teams**.
5. Add the project to a relevant Teams channel for collaboration.

Tip: Use the **Planner tab** in Teams for task management alongside your project plan.

3.2 Syncing with SharePoint

1. Save the project file to SharePoint:
   - Navigate to **File > Save As > SharePoint**.
   - Choose your SharePoint site and folder.
2. Share the file link with team members.
3. Enable version control to track changes.

Benefits:

- Centralized storage and accessibility.
- Real-time updates for collaborators.

3.3 Integrating with Outlook

1. Go to **Task Information** in Microsoft Project.
2. Assign tasks to team members with Outlook email addresses.
3. Sync project deadlines with calendars:
   - Export tasks to Outlook via **Task Pane > Export > Outlook**.
4. Use reminders for upcoming deadlines.

3.4 Utilizing OneDrive for File Sharing

1. Save the project file to OneDrive:
   - Navigate to **File > Save As > OneDrive**.
   - Share the link with stakeholders.
2. Enable collaborative editing by granting edit permissions.

3.5 Power BI for Reporting

1. Export project data to Power BI:
   - Navigate to **File > Export > Power BI**.
2. Create interactive dashboards using:
   - Gantt charts.
   - Critical path analyses.
   - Resource allocation trends.

4. Automating Workflows with Microsoft 365

4.1 Automating Tasks with Power Automate

- Create custom workflows between Microsoft Project and other 365 tools:
  - Example: Automatically send task updates to Teams channels.
  - Steps:
    1. Log in to **Power Automate**.
    2. Select a template, such as "Notify Teams when a task is updated in Project."
    3. Customize triggers and actions.

4.2 Linking with Planner

- Use Planner for detailed task management.
- Steps:
    1. Export tasks from Microsoft Project to Planner.
    2. Link Planner boards to Teams for visibility.

5. Best Practices for Synchronization

5.1 Regular Updates

- Ensure project files are synced daily to avoid discrepancies.

5.2 Access Permissions

- Restrict permissions to maintain data security and confidentiality.

5.3 Clear Communication

- Inform team members about synced updates and changes.

5.4 Training

- Provide training on using Microsoft 365 tools effectively with Project.

6. Troubleshooting Common Issues

Issue 1: Sync Delays

- **Solution**: Check internet connectivity and server settings.

Issue 2: Duplicate Tasks

- **Solution**: Regularly review and reconcile data to remove duplicates.

Issue 3: Integration Failures

- **Solution**: Update Microsoft Project and 365 tools to the latest versions.

7. Summary

Synchronizing Microsoft Project with Microsoft 365 tools unlocks the full potential of project management. From real-time collaboration with Teams to advanced reporting in Power BI, integration streamlines workflows and ensures projects are delivered on time.

Key Takeaways:

- Utilize Microsoft Teams for collaboration and communication.
- Leverage SharePoint and OneDrive for centralized file management.
- Automate workflows with Power Automate for efficiency.

In the next chapter, we will explore **Coordinating with Project Online or Project Server** for managing enterprise-level projects.

Coordinating with Project Online or Project Server

Effective project management often involves collaboration across teams and departments, making tools like **Project Online** and **Project Server** indispensable for centralized project coordination. These platforms are built to integrate seamlessly with Microsoft Project, enabling advanced project management capabilities such as resource pooling, cross-project dependencies, and robust reporting. This chapter provides a comprehensive guide on how to coordinate with these tools effectively.

1. Understanding Project Online and Project Server

1.1 What is Project Online?

- A cloud-based service within Microsoft 365 that allows for enterprise-level project and portfolio management.
- Features include project scheduling, resource management, and portfolio optimization.
- Accessible from anywhere, supporting real-time collaboration.

1.2 What is Project Server?

- An on-premises solution for enterprise project management.
- Provides similar features as Project Online but is hosted within your organization's IT infrastructure.
- Offers greater control over data but requires internal IT resources for maintenance.

2. Benefits of Using Project Online or Project Server

2.1 Centralized Project Management

- Consolidates all projects into a single platform.
- Enables cross-project visibility for better decision-making.

2.2 Enhanced Collaboration

- Facilitates team collaboration through integration with Microsoft Teams, SharePoint, and OneDrive.
- Real-time updates ensure all stakeholders have the latest project data.

2.3 Resource Optimization

- Allows resource pooling and tracking across multiple projects.
- Reduces overallocation and ensures efficient resource utilization.

2.4 Robust Reporting

- Provides pre-built and custom reporting options.
- Integrates with Power BI for advanced analytics.

2.5 Scalability

- Both tools support organizations of all sizes, from small teams to large enterprises.

3. Setting Up Project Online

3.1 Accessing Project Online

1. Log in to Microsoft 365 and navigate to **Project Online**.
2. Select **Create New Project** to start a project or **Import** an existing one.

3.2 Connecting Microsoft Project to Project Online

1. Open Microsoft Project and go to **File > Account Settings**.
2. Enter your Project Online URL and login credentials.
3. Save your settings to enable direct synchronization.

3.3 Configuring Permissions

- Assign roles such as Project Manager, Team Member, and Portfolio Manager.
- Use Microsoft 365 Admin Center to manage permissions.

3.4 Uploading a Project Plan

1. Finalize the project plan in Microsoft Project.
2. Navigate to **File > Save As > Project Online**.
3. Choose a site and library to upload the project file.

---

4. Setting Up Project Server

4.1 Installation and Configuration

- Work with your IT team to install Project Server on the organization's server.
- Configure the application using the **SharePoint Central Administration Tool**.

4.2 Connecting Microsoft Project to Project Server

1. Open Microsoft Project and navigate to **File > Info > Manage Accounts**.
2. Select **Add** and enter the Project Server URL.
3. Save and set this account as the default.

4.3 Publishing a Project

1. Go to **File > Save As > Project Server**.
2. Choose the appropriate enterprise project template.
3. Publish the project for organization-wide visibility.

---

5. Key Features for Coordination

5.1 Resource Pooling

- Create a centralized pool of resources for allocation across projects.
- Track resource availability and utilization.

5.2 Task Delegation

- Assign tasks to team members directly from Project Online or Server.
- Monitor task progress using real-time updates.

5.3 Cross-Project Dependencies

- Link tasks between projects to manage dependencies effectively.
- Use the **Master Project** feature for oversight of interconnected projects.

5.4 Reporting and Dashboards

- Access pre-built reports, such as Project Overview, Resource Workload, and Cost Analysis.
- Create custom dashboards using Power BI.

---

6. Best Practices for Coordinating with Project Online or Server

6.1 Regular Updates

- Ensure project data is updated frequently to reflect the latest progress.

6.2 Data Consistency

- Standardize naming conventions and project templates to maintain consistency.

6.3 Permissions Management

- Grant appropriate access levels to ensure data security.

6.4 Training and Onboarding

- Train team members on how to use Project Online or Server effectively.

6.5 Backup and Recovery

- Regularly back up project data to prevent loss during server failures or outages.

---

7. Troubleshooting Common Issues

7.1 Connectivity Problems

- **Solution**: Verify internet connection for Project Online or server settings for Project Server.

7.2 Sync Failures

- **Solution**: Check for conflicts between local and online data and resolve them.

7.3 Resource Allocation Errors

- **Solution**: Use the Resource Center to review and adjust allocations.

Summary: Coordinating with Project Online or Project Server ensures seamless project management across an organization. Whether your team operates on-premises or in the cloud, these tools provide robust features for resource management, cross-project dependencies, and real-time collaboration.

Key Takeaways:

- Use Project Online for cloud-based project management and remote access.
- Opt for Project Server for on-premises control and customization.
- Leverage features like resource pooling, task delegation, and reporting for effective coordination.

In the next chapter, we will explore **Communicating Project Updates to Stakeholders**, focusing on strategies to ensure timely and transparent communication.

Communicating Project Updates to Stakeholders

Effective communication is critical for project success. Keeping stakeholders informed ensures alignment, builds trust, and helps in managing expectations throughout the project lifecycle. Microsoft Project offers robust tools and features that make it easy to track progress and share updates with stakeholders in a structured and professional manner.

1. Importance of Stakeholder Communication

1.1 Building Trust and Transparency

- Open communication fosters trust between the project team and stakeholders.
- Regular updates ensure everyone has a clear understanding of project status, risks, and milestones.

1.2 Managing Expectations

- Timely communication helps address concerns and reduces the chances of misunderstandings.
- Proactive updates mitigate the risk of surprise delays or budget overruns.

1.3 Facilitating Decision-Making

- Clear reporting enables stakeholders to make informed decisions.
- Provides an opportunity to discuss and resolve issues collaboratively.

2. Features in Microsoft Project for Stakeholder Communication

2.1 Visual Reporting Tools

- **Gantt Charts**: Simplify complex project data for easy visualization.
- **Timeline View**: Presents high-level project overviews for quick understanding.
- **Dashboard Reports**: Provide key performance indicators (KPIs) and project summaries.

2.2 Collaborative Tools

- **Export to SharePoint or Project Online**: Share real-time project data with stakeholders.
- **Integration with Microsoft Teams**: Use Teams to present project updates and facilitate discussions.
- **Email Integration**: Share reports and schedules directly via email.

2.3 Customizable Reports

- Use built-in and custom reports to tailor updates to stakeholder needs.
- Highlight critical information such as milestones, budget usage, and task progress.

3. Preparing for Stakeholder Communication

3.1 Identifying Stakeholder Needs

- Understand what each stakeholder values most in project updates (e.g., financial data, timelines, risks).

- Create a communication matrix to track the frequency and format of updates for each stakeholder group.

3.2 Choosing the Right Format

- Use **Presentations** for formal meetings with executives.
- Share **Dashboards and Reports** for team and department-level updates.
- Provide **Detailed Task Lists** for operational-level stakeholders.

3.3 Setting a Communication Schedule

- Schedule regular updates (e.g., weekly, biweekly, or monthly).
- Align updates with project milestones to provide meaningful insights.

---

4. Sharing Updates Using Microsoft Project

4.1 Using the Timeline View

1. Navigate to the **Timeline** tab in the ribbon.
2. Highlight key tasks, milestones, and deadlines.
3. Export the timeline as an image or integrate it into PowerPoint for presentations.

4.2 Generating Reports

1. Go to the **Report** tab in Microsoft Project.
2. Select from pre-built reports such as:
    - **Project Overview**: A high-level snapshot of project health.
    - **Cost Overview**: Insights into budget and expenditure.
    - **Milestone Report**: A detailed view of key milestones and their statuses.
3. Customize reports to include specific charts, tables, or visuals relevant to stakeholders.

4.3 Exporting Data

- **Excel**: Use Excel for stakeholders who prefer detailed data analysis.
- **PDF**: Generate PDFs for professional-looking static reports.
- **SharePoint or Project Online**: Provide real-time access to project files and updates.

---

5. Tips for Effective Communication

5.1 Simplify the Message

- Avoid technical jargon; use visuals and plain language to convey key points.
- Focus on high-impact information that aligns with stakeholder interests.

5.2 Address Risks and Challenges

- Be transparent about potential risks and ongoing challenges.
- Present solutions or action plans to demonstrate control over the situation.

5.3 Highlight Successes

- Celebrate milestones and achievements to build confidence in the project team.
- Use progress charts or "before-and-after" comparisons to showcase improvements.

5.4 Encourage Feedback

- Create opportunities for stakeholders to ask questions and provide input.
- Use surveys or feedback forms to gauge satisfaction and gather suggestions.

---

6. Case Study: Stakeholder Update Workflow

Scenario: A software development project with diverse stakeholders including executives, team leads, and clients.

Step 1: Plan Communication

- Weekly email updates for executives with budget and milestone summaries.
- Biweekly team meetings to discuss task-level progress.
- Monthly dashboards for clients showcasing timeline progress and deliverables.

Step 2: Generate Reports

- Create a **Milestone Report** for executives using Microsoft Project.
- Use the **Task Progress Report** for team discussions.
- Share a **Timeline View** with clients for visual representation of progress.

Step 3: Share Updates

- Upload reports to SharePoint for real-time access.
- Schedule virtual meetings via Microsoft Teams for interactive discussions.
- Provide follow-up emails summarizing key points discussed during meetings.

---

7. Overcoming Common Communication Challenges

7.1 Dealing with Misaligned Expectations

- **Solution**: Use clear and consistent reporting formats. Align updates with the project scope and goals.

7.2 Managing Stakeholder Availability

- **Solution**: Use asynchronous tools like SharePoint and email to accommodate different schedules.

7.3 Handling Negative Feedback

- **Solution**: Approach feedback constructively by focusing on actionable solutions.

---

8. Summary

Communicating effectively with stakeholders is a cornerstone of successful project management. By leveraging Microsoft Project's robust tools and tailoring updates to stakeholder needs, project managers can foster transparency, trust, and alignment throughout the project lifecycle.

Key Takeaways:

- Use tools like Gantt Charts, Timeline View, and Reports for impactful communication.
- Customize updates based on stakeholder priorities and preferences.

- Encourage two-way communication to ensure alignment and build trust.

In the next chapter, we'll delve into **Working with Master Projects**, exploring techniques to manage multiple projects effectively using Microsoft Project.

Section X:
Multiple Projects and Advanced Techniques

Working with Master Projects

Managing multiple projects simultaneously can be a daunting task without the right tools and techniques. Microsoft Project provides a robust solution for integrating and managing multiple projects through the use of master projects. A master project allows you to consolidate several individual project plans into a single file, enabling you to oversee and coordinate complex, interrelated efforts effectively.

---

1. Understanding Master Projects

1.1 What is a Master Project?

- A **master project** acts as a central repository, containing multiple subprojects within it.
- Each subproject remains a separate file, but its data is accessible and manageable from the master project.

1.2 Benefits of Using a Master Project

- **Centralized Management**: View and manage all projects from a single file.
- **Enhanced Coordination**: Easily identify dependencies and relationships between projects.
- **Improved Reporting**: Generate consolidated reports that provide a comprehensive overview of all projects.
- **Efficient Resource Allocation**: Manage and resolve resource conflicts across projects.

---

2. Creating a Master Project

2.1 Preparing Subprojects

Before creating a master project, ensure that:

- All subprojects are finalized and saved as individual files.
- Resource names are consistent across all subprojects to avoid duplication or confusion.
- Subprojects are saved in accessible locations for linking.

2.2 Steps to Create a Master Project

1. **Open Microsoft Project** and create a new blank project.
2. **Insert Subprojects**:
   - Navigate to the **Project** tab in the ribbon.
   - Click **Subproject** and select the project files you want to include.
   - Check the option for **Link to project** to maintain a dynamic connection between the master and subprojects.
3. **Review the Structure**:
   - Each subproject will appear as a summary task within the master project.
   - Expand or collapse subprojects as needed to view or hide task details.

3. Managing Subprojects in a Master Project

3.1 Updating Subprojects

- Changes made to tasks or schedules in a subproject will automatically reflect in the master project if they are linked.
- Conversely, updates in the master project will propagate back to the subprojects.

3.2 Adjusting Dependencies

- Link tasks between subprojects to define dependencies.
  - Select a task from one subproject, and then link it to a task in another using the **Predecessors** column or the **Task Dependencies** dialog.

3.3 Resolving Resource Conflicts

- Use the **Resource Usage** view to identify and resolve overallocations across projects.
- Adjust assignments or resource availability directly within the master project.

4. Best Practices for Working with Master Projects

4.1 Maintain Subproject Autonomy

- Keep subprojects modular and manageable by their respective teams.
- Avoid making unnecessary changes to individual subprojects through the master project.

4.2 Use Consistent File Management

- Save all subprojects and the master project in the same directory to prevent broken links.
- Use clear naming conventions for project files.

4.3 Regularly Update Links

- Ensure all subproject links are up-to-date to reflect the latest changes.
- Periodically review the master project for outdated or broken links.

4.4 Back Up Files

- Create regular backups of the master project and its subprojects to prevent data loss.

5. Reporting Across a Master Project

5.1 Generating Consolidated Reports

- Use built-in reports like **Project Overview** or **Milestone Report** for a high-level summary.
- Customize reports to include data from all subprojects.

5.2 Tracking Progress

- View the overall progress of tasks and milestones across all subprojects in the **Gantt Chart** view.
- Use the **Timeline** view to present key deliverables from all projects.

5.3 Monitoring Resource Allocation

- Access the **Resource Graph** to visualize workloads and availability across projects.

---

6. Common Challenges and Solutions

6.1 Broken Links Between Projects

- **Challenge**: Moving or renaming subproject files may break their links to the master project.
- **Solution**: Use the **Information** dialog to update the file paths of subprojects.

6.2 Overlapping Dependencies

- **Challenge**: Tasks in different subprojects may have conflicting schedules or dependencies.
- **Solution**: Use the **Task Inspector** to identify and adjust conflicting dependencies.

6.3 Resource Overallocations

- **Challenge**: Shared resources may become overallocated across subprojects.
- **Solution**: Use the **Resource Leveling** tool to distribute workloads more evenly.

---

7. Summary

Master projects provide a powerful way to manage multiple projects efficiently by consolidating them into a single file. They offer centralized visibility, enhanced coordination, and better resource management across interconnected efforts. By following best practices and leveraging Microsoft Project's features, project managers can navigate the complexities of multi-project management with confidence.

Key Takeaways:

- Master projects enable a consolidated view of multiple subprojects while maintaining their independence.
- Use task linking and resource sharing to coordinate and optimize project efforts.
- Regular updates and consistent file management are essential for successful multi-project management.

In the next chapter, we will explore **Using Subprojects and Linked Projects**, diving deeper into techniques for managing project dependencies and maintaining flexibility across linked plans.

Using Subprojects and Linked Projects

Managing a complex project portfolio often requires breaking down larger initiatives into smaller, more manageable components. Microsoft Project supports this with subprojects and linked projects, allowing teams to maintain autonomy while integrating their efforts into a cohesive whole. This chapter will explore the process of working with subprojects and establishing links between projects to achieve seamless coordination.

1. Understanding Subprojects and Linked Projects

1.1 What are Subprojects?

- Subprojects are individual project files that are integrated into a larger **master project**.
- Each subproject retains its independence, making it manageable by separate teams while contributing to the overarching project goals.

1.2 What are Linked Projects?

- Linked projects are independent project files that share interdependencies, such as task relationships or shared resources.
- Linking projects enables you to align schedules, milestones, and deliverables across multiple efforts.

1.3 Benefits of Subprojects and Linked Projects

- **Scalability**: Manage complex programs by dividing them into smaller, focused projects.
- **Flexibility**: Allow independent updates to subprojects while maintaining integration.
- **Coordination**: Streamline collaboration by aligning dependencies and resources across linked projects.

2. Working with Subprojects

2.1 Creating Subprojects

- Save each component of the larger initiative as an individual project file.
- Clearly define the scope, resources, and tasks for each subproject to avoid duplication or conflicts.

2.2 Inserting Subprojects into a Master Project

1. Open the master project file or create a new one.
2. Go to the **Project** tab and click on **Subproject**.
3. Select the subproject files to include and check the **Link to project** option.
4. Click **Insert** to add the subprojects as summary tasks in the master project.

2.3 Managing Subprojects in the Master Project

- Expand or collapse the subproject summary tasks to view or hide their details.
- Update subproject schedules and tasks as necessary; linked subprojects will reflect these changes automatically.

3. Linking Projects

3.1 Creating Links Between Tasks Across Projects

1. Open both project files you want to link.
2. In the **Task** tab, select the task in one project that will serve as the predecessor.
3. Copy the task ID or navigate to the destination project.
4. Paste the predecessor ID into the **Predecessors** column of the dependent task.

3.2 Viewing and Managing Linked Tasks

- Use the **Task Information** dialog to review and modify linked tasks.
- Linked tasks will display external predecessor or successor indicators.

3.3 Resolving Scheduling Conflicts

- Use the **Task Inspector** to identify and address issues such as overlapping schedules or resource overallocations caused by linked tasks.

---

4. Best Practices for Using Subprojects and Linked Projects

4.1 Define Clear Project Boundaries

- Establish the scope, tasks, and deliverables of each subproject before integration to minimize confusion.

4.2 Use Consistent Resource Naming

- Avoid duplicate resource names across projects by using a standardized naming convention.

4.3 Maintain Logical Task Links

- Only link tasks that have clear dependencies to prevent unnecessary complexity.

4.4 Regularly Update and Sync Projects

- Ensure changes in subprojects or linked projects are synchronized to maintain accurate data in the master project.

4.5 Use Descriptive File Names

- Save project files with descriptive names to make them easily identifiable in the master project.

---

5. Troubleshooting Common Challenges

5.1 Broken Links

- **Problem**: Moving or renaming linked project files breaks the connection.
- **Solution**: Use the **Information** dialog to update the file paths for the linked projects.

5.2 Scheduling Conflicts

- **Problem**: Dependencies between tasks in linked projects create conflicts.
- **Solution**: Adjust task constraints, durations, or dependency types to resolve the conflicts.

5.3 Resource Overallocations

- **Problem**: Shared resources across linked projects become overallocated.
- **Solution**: Use the **Resource Usage** view to balance workloads or adjust resource assignments.

---

6. Reporting Across Subprojects and Linked Projects

6.1 Consolidated Reporting in Master Projects

- Generate reports in the master project to view combined progress, costs, and schedules for all subprojects.

6.2 Tracking Dependencies Across Projects

- Use the **Task Path** feature to visualize dependencies between tasks across linked projects.

6.3 Monitoring Resource Utilization

- Access the **Resource Graph** or **Resource Sheet** views to analyze resource availability and allocation.

---

7. Summary

Subprojects and linked projects offer powerful ways to manage and coordinate complex programs. By integrating multiple project files, Microsoft Project enables teams to balance individual autonomy with centralized oversight. Following best practices and leveraging features like task linking and consolidated reporting can help project managers maintain alignment and achieve success across interconnected efforts.

Key Takeaways:

- Subprojects simplify management by breaking large programs into smaller, focused components.
- Linked projects establish dependencies and resource sharing between independent efforts.
- Regular updates and synchronized files ensure the accuracy and reliability of master projects.

In the next chapter, we will discuss **Setting Up Cross-Project Dependencies**, exploring how to effectively align schedules and resources across multiple interdependent projects.

Setting Up Cross-Project Dependencies

Managing large-scale initiatives often involves multiple interconnected projects. Establishing cross-project dependencies ensures alignment between schedules, tasks, and resources. This chapter guides you through the process of setting up and managing cross-project dependencies in Microsoft Project to maintain coherence across interdependent projects.

1. Understanding Cross-Project Dependencies

1.1 What are Cross-Project Dependencies?

- **Definition**: Cross-project dependencies are links between tasks in different project files. These dependencies ensure that changes in one project automatically update related tasks in another.
- **Purpose**: They help synchronize schedules, resources, and deliverables across multiple projects.

1.2 Types of Cross-Project Dependencies

- **Finish-to-Start (FS)**: One task must finish before the dependent task starts.
- **Start-to-Start (SS)**: Two tasks start at the same time.
- **Finish-to-Finish (FF)**: Two tasks finish simultaneously.
- **Start-to-Finish (SF)**: One task cannot finish until another task starts.

2. Preparing to Establish Dependencies

2.1 Define Project Boundaries

- Clearly identify the scope and tasks of each project to avoid overlap and confusion.

2.2 Use a Centralized Resource Pool (Optional)

- Consider using a shared resource pool to streamline resource allocation across projects. This reduces the risk of overallocation or duplication.

2.3 Save and Organize Files

- Save all project files in a central location to make linking tasks easier. Use descriptive file names to identify projects quickly.

3. Setting Up Cross-Project Dependencies

3.1 Linking Tasks Across Projects

1. **Open Both Projects**: Open the project files containing the tasks you want to link.
2. **Identify the Tasks**: Determine the predecessor task in the first project and the dependent task in the second project.
3. **Create the Link**:
   - In the **Task** tab, select the predecessor task in the first project.
   - Copy the task ID or click **Task Information** to view the task details.
   - Switch to the second project and locate the dependent task.
   - In the **Predecessors** column, input the file name and task ID of the predecessor task (e.g., [Project1].mpp\3).

3.2 Verifying Links

- Check that the dependency is correctly established by reviewing the **Task Information** or **Predecessors** fields.
- Use the **Task Path** feature to visualize the dependency relationship.

---

4. Managing Cross-Project Dependencies

4.1 Handling Changes

- **Rescheduling Predecessors**: Changes in the predecessor task automatically update the dependent task's schedule.
- **Notification of Changes**: Microsoft Project notifies you of any updates or conflicts in linked tasks.

4.2 Breaking Dependencies

- If a dependency is no longer needed:
    - Open the dependent project.
    - Delete the predecessor task ID from the **Predecessors** column.

4.3 Resolving Conflicts

- **Conflict Detection**: Use the **Task Inspector** to identify and resolve issues caused by dependencies, such as scheduling conflicts or resource overallocations.
- **Adjusting Links**: Modify the dependency type or task durations to resolve conflicts.

---

5. Best Practices for Cross-Project Dependencies

5.1 Keep Dependencies Logical

- Only create dependencies for tasks that truly rely on each other to minimize unnecessary complexity.

5.2 Regularly Update Projects

- Ensure all linked projects are regularly updated to maintain accurate schedules and task relationships.

5.3 Use Descriptive Task Names

- Assign clear and descriptive names to tasks involved in dependencies for easier identification.

5.4 Document Dependency Relationships

- Maintain a list of cross-project dependencies to track relationships and dependencies across projects.

---

6. Reporting on Cross-Project Dependencies

6.1 Using Consolidated Reporting

- Combine multiple project files into a **master project** to generate reports that include cross-project dependencies.

- Use the **Gantt Chart** or **Timeline View** in the master project to visualize relationships.

6.2 Monitoring Linked Tasks

- Use the **Predecessor Successor Report** to identify and analyze all linked tasks across projects.

6.3 Resource Analysis

- Check the **Resource Usage** view to monitor resource allocations affected by cross-project dependencies.

---

7. Troubleshooting Common Challenges

7.1 Broken Links

- **Problem**: Moving or renaming project files breaks dependency links.
- **Solution**: Update the file path for the predecessor task in the **Task Information** dialog.

7.2 Circular Dependencies

- **Problem**: Two tasks create a loop where neither can be scheduled.
- **Solution**: Reevaluate task relationships to eliminate circular dependencies.

7.3 Overallocations

- **Problem**: Dependencies cause overlapping resource assignments.
- **Solution**: Adjust task schedules or reallocate resources using the **Resource Leveling** tool.

---

8. Summary

Cross-project dependencies play a vital role in managing complex, interrelated projects. By carefully linking tasks and monitoring their relationships, you can ensure seamless coordination across your portfolio. Following best practices and utilizing Microsoft Project's tools for dependency management will help you maintain control and achieve success in multi-project environments.

Key Takeaways:

- Establish dependencies only when tasks are genuinely interrelated.
- Regularly update and monitor linked tasks to avoid conflicts.
- Use consolidated reporting to analyze and visualize cross-project relationships.

In the next chapter, we'll explore **Managing Resource Pools Across Projects**, focusing on how to allocate and balance resources effectively across a portfolio.

Managing Resource Pools Across Projects

Efficient resource management is critical when dealing with multiple projects. Sharing resources across projects ensures optimal utilization, minimizes conflicts, and streamlines project execution. This chapter focuses on managing resource pools in Microsoft Project to effectively allocate, track, and optimize resources across a portfolio of projects.

1. Understanding Resource Pools

1.1 What is a Resource Pool?

- A **resource pool** is a centralized repository of resources (people, equipment, or materials) shared among multiple projects.
- By linking projects to a resource pool, you can:
  - Track resource availability.
  - Avoid overallocations.
  - Maintain consistency in resource rates and calendars.

1.2 Benefits of Using a Resource Pool

- **Centralized Management**: All resources are managed from a single location.
- **Real-Time Updates**: Changes in resource assignments or availability automatically reflect in all linked projects.
- **Conflict Resolution**: Easily identify and address resource overallocations across projects.

2. Setting Up a Resource Pool

2.1 Creating a Resource Pool

1. Open Microsoft Project and create a new project file.
2. Go to the **Resource Sheet View**:
   - Click **View** > **Resource Sheet**.
3. Add resources to the sheet:
   - Enter resource names, types (work, material, or cost), and availability details.
4. Save the project file as your resource pool (e.g., ResourcePool.mpp).

2.2 Linking Projects to the Resource Pool

1. Open the resource pool file and the project files you want to link.
2. In the project file:
   - Go to **Resource** > **Resource Pool** > **Share Resources**.
   - Select **Use Resources From** and choose the resource pool file.
3. Save all files after linking.

3. Allocating Resources from the Pool

3.1 Assigning Shared Resources

- After linking to the resource pool, assign resources to tasks in your project:
  - Go to **Gantt Chart View**.

- Select a task and open the **Task Information** dialog.
- Assign a resource from the shared pool.

3.2 Monitoring Resource Usage

- Use the **Resource Usage View**:
  - Go to **View > Resource Usage**.
  - Review resource assignments across linked projects to ensure balance.

---

4. Resolving Overallocations

4.1 Identifying Overallocations

- Overallocations occur when a resource is assigned more work than available during a given time period.
- View overallocations in:
  - **Resource Sheet**: Overallocated resources appear in red.
  - **Team Planner View**: Displays a visual representation of overallocated tasks.

4.2 Resolving Overallocations

1. **Adjust Task Schedules**: Use the **Level Resource** tool:
   - Go to **Resource > Level Resource**.
   - Select the overallocated resource and adjust schedules.
2. **Reassign Tasks**: Shift tasks to other available resources.
3. **Modify Work Durations**: Extend task durations to reduce workload.

---

5. Maintaining the Resource Pool

5.1 Updating Resource Information

- Regularly update the resource pool with:
  - Changes in resource availability.
  - New resources or adjustments to existing resource rates.
  - Updated calendars for holidays or time off.

5.2 Managing Changes Across Linked Projects

- Changes made in the resource pool automatically propagate to linked projects.
- Save and close all linked files after updates to ensure synchronization.

---

6. Viewing and Reporting Resource Pool Data

6.1 Analyzing Resource Allocation

- Use the **Resource Graph**:
  - Go to **View > Resource Graph** to see resource workloads.
- Review availability using the **Resource Availability Table**.

6.2 Generating Reports

- Generate reports to monitor resource usage across projects:

○ Go to **Report** > **Resource Reports** > **Resource Overview** or **Resource Usage**.

7. Best Practices for Managing Resource Pools

7.1 Use Consistent Resource Naming

- Ensure resources have consistent and descriptive names to avoid duplication or confusion.

7.2 Save Resource Pool Separately

- Save the resource pool file in a secure, accessible location to prevent accidental changes.

7.3 Regularly Update Resource Data

- Keep resource availability, rates, and calendars up-to-date to maintain accuracy.

7.4 Monitor Resource Utilization

- Frequently review resource workloads to identify and address issues early.

7.5 Communicate Changes

- Notify team members and stakeholders of changes in resource assignments or availability.

8. Troubleshooting Common Issues

8.1 Broken Links to the Resource Pool

- **Problem**: Linked projects cannot access the resource pool.
- **Solution**: Re-link the project to the resource pool using **Share Resources**.

8.2 Conflicting Updates

- **Problem**: Multiple users make changes to the resource pool simultaneously.
- **Solution**: Designate a single person to manage the resource pool or use a version control system.

9. Summary

Managing a shared resource pool across projects enhances efficiency, improves visibility, and ensures balanced workloads. By following the steps outlined in this chapter, you can effectively allocate and track resources, resolve conflicts, and maintain project alignment.

Key Takeaways:

- Use a centralized resource pool for better control and visibility.
- Regularly update and monitor resource data to avoid overallocations.
- Utilize Microsoft Project's tools for resource reporting and analysis.

In the next chapter, we will explore **Adding and Configuring Custom Fields**, a powerful way to track additional project data and tailor Microsoft Project to your specific needs.

Section XI:
Custom Fields and Automation

Adding and Configuring Custom Fields

Custom fields in Microsoft Project allow you to tailor your project data to meet specific requirements. They enable enhanced tracking, reporting, and management by capturing information beyond the standard fields. This chapter provides a comprehensive guide on creating, configuring, and utilizing custom fields effectively.

1. Introduction to Custom Fields

1.1 What Are Custom Fields?

- **Custom fields** are user-defined fields that you can add to Microsoft Project to capture unique project information.
- Examples include:
    - Project priorities.
    - Risk levels.
    - Custom calculations.

1.2 Types of Custom Fields

Microsoft Project offers the following types of custom fields:

- **Text**: Stores alphanumeric values.
- **Number**: Captures numeric data.
- **Date**: Tracks specific dates.
- **Duration**: Measures time spans.
- **Flag**: Boolean fields for Yes/No.
- **Cost**: Holds cost-related information.

2. Creating Custom Fields

2.1 Accessing Custom Fields

1. Navigate to the **Project tab**.
2. Select **Custom Fields** under the **Properties** group.

2.2 Steps to Create a Custom Field

1. In the **Custom Fields** dialog box:
    - Select the **Field Type** (e.g., Text, Number).
    - Choose a specific **Field Name** from the list (e.g., Text1, Number2).
2. Click **Rename** to provide a meaningful name for the field.
    - Example: Rename Text1 to "Priority Level."
3. Optionally, add a **Formula** or **Lookup Table** for advanced functionality.

2.3 Customizing Field Properties

- Set a **Default Value** for the field to save time during data entry.
- Enable **Calculation for Summary Rows** to display aggregated values in summary tasks.

---

3. Using Lookup Tables for Custom Fields

3.1 What Are Lookup Tables?

- Lookup tables allow predefined values for custom fields, ensuring consistency and accuracy.
- Example: A "Risk Level" field with options: High, Medium, Low.

3.2 Creating a Lookup Table

1. In the **Custom Fields** dialog, click **Lookup**.
2. Add predefined values:
   - Enter each value (e.g., High, Medium, Low).
   - Set a default value if needed.
3. Save the lookup table and apply it to the custom field.

---

4. Configuring Formulas for Advanced Tracking

4.1 Why Use Formulas?

- Formulas in custom fields allow dynamic calculations based on existing project data.
- Example: Automatically calculate a task's risk score using duration and cost.

4.2 Creating a Formula

1. In the **Custom Fields** dialog, select the target field.
2. Click **Formula** and enter the calculation:
   - Use available functions like IIf, DateDiff, Abs.
   - Example Formula:

```
IIf([Duration]>10, "High", "Low")
```

   - This sets a "High" value if the task duration exceeds 10 days.

4.3 Validating and Testing

- After adding a formula, test it by applying it to tasks and verifying the results.

---

5. Displaying Custom Fields in Views

5.1 Adding Custom Fields to Views

1. Navigate to the desired view (e.g., **Gantt Chart**).
2. Right-click on a column header and select **Insert Column**.
3. Choose your custom field from the list.

5.2 Formatting Custom Fields

- Adjust column width and alignment for better visibility.
- Use conditional formatting to highlight specific values.

5.3 Filtering and Sorting by Custom Fields

- Apply filters or sorting rules based on custom field values to prioritize or group tasks.

---

6. Applying Custom Fields in Reports

6.1 Using Custom Fields in Built-In Reports

1. Go to the **Report** tab.
2. Select a report (e.g., **Task Overview**).
3. Customize the report by adding your custom fields.

6.2 Creating a Custom Report

- Include custom fields in tables, charts, or dashboards for advanced insights.

---

7. Best Practices for Custom Fields

7.1 Keep Names Descriptive

- Use clear, descriptive names for custom fields to avoid confusion.

7.2 Limit the Number of Custom Fields

- Only create custom fields that add significant value to your project tracking.

7.3 Document Custom Fields

- Maintain documentation for custom fields, including their purpose, formulas, and lookup tables.

7.4 Test Before Deployment

- Test custom fields in a sample project before applying them across multiple projects.

---

8. Troubleshooting Common Issues

8.1 Custom Field Not Updating

- **Solution**: Check if the field is set to calculate values manually or requires input.

8.2 Incorrect Formula Results

- **Solution**: Verify the formula syntax and logic. Test with different scenarios.

8.3 Lookup Values Not Displaying

- **Solution**: Ensure the custom field is correctly linked to the lookup table.

---

9. Summary

Custom fields are a powerful feature in Microsoft Project, enabling you to capture and analyze data unique to your project's needs. By mastering custom fields, you can create a tailored project management experience, enhance tracking capabilities, and generate more insightful reports.

Key Takeaways:

- Use custom fields to capture unique project data.
- Leverage formulas and lookup tables for advanced functionality.
- Display and filter custom fields in views and reports for better project insights.

In the next chapter, we will explore **Leveraging Formulas for Advanced Tracking**, diving deeper into complex calculations and data analysis within Microsoft Project.

Leveraging Formulas for Advanced Tracking

Formulas in Microsoft Project allow for advanced customization and automation by enabling calculations based on project data. They are a powerful tool for project managers looking to enhance tracking and decision-making capabilities. This chapter will guide you through creating and applying formulas to maximize the effectiveness of your project tracking.

1. Understanding Formulas in Microsoft Project

1.1 What Are Formulas?

- Formulas are user-defined expressions that perform calculations based on project data.
- They can dynamically generate values in custom fields, enhancing your ability to monitor and analyze project performance.

1.2 Benefits of Using Formulas

- Automates repetitive calculations.
- Customizes tracking metrics.
- Generates insights specific to your project requirements.

1.3 Limitations

- Formulas apply only to custom fields.
- Calculations are limited to the scope of available project data and functions.

2. Creating Formulas

2.1 Accessing the Formula Editor

1. Go to the **Project** tab.
2. Select **Custom Fields** under the **Properties** group.
3. In the **Custom Fields** dialog, select the desired field type (e.g., Text, Number).
4. Click the **Formula** button to open the editor.

2.2 Building a Formula

- Use a combination of project field names, operators, and functions.
- Example: To calculate the remaining budget for a task:
  ```
  [Budget] - [Actual Cost]
  ```
- Copy

2.3 Testing Formulas

- After creating a formula, apply it to tasks and verify the accuracy of the calculations.
- Ensure the formula accounts for edge cases (e.g., null or zero values).

3. Common Use Cases for Formulas

3.1 Risk Scoring

- Calculate a task's risk score based on duration and cost:
  ```
  IIf([Duration] > 10 And [Cost] > 1000, "High", "Low")
  ```
- Copy
- Result: Tasks exceeding 10 days and $1,000 are marked as "High Risk."

3.2 Custom Percent Complete

- Derive a weighted percent complete for a task:
  ```
  ([Work] * [Percent Complete]) / [Baseline Work]
  ```
- Copy
- This provides a more nuanced view of progress based on actual work.

3.3 Calculating Slack

- Display slack time as a custom field:
  ```
  [Finish Slack] / [Minutes Per Day]
  ```
- Copy
- Converts slack time from minutes to days for easier interpretation.

---

4. Using Functions in Formulas

4.1 Logical Functions

- **IIf(condition, true_value, false_value)**: Conditional logic.
  - Example: Highlight overdue tasks:
    ```
    IIf([Finish] < Now(), "Overdue", "On Track")
    ```
  - Copy

4.2 Mathematical Functions

- **Abs(number)**: Absolute value.
- **Round(number, digits)**: Rounds numbers to a specified number of digits.
  - Example: Round off remaining work:
    ```
    Round([Remaining Work], 2)
    ```
  - Copy

4.3 Date and Time Functions

- **DateDiff(interval, date1, date2)**: Calculates the difference between two dates.
  - Example: Days until task completion:
    ```
    DateDiff("d", Now(), [Finish])
    ```
  - Copy

---

5. Applying Formulas to Custom Fields

5.1 Assigning to a Field

- Once a formula is created, it is automatically assigned to the selected custom field.
- Add the custom field as a column in your desired view for easy reference.

5.2 Aggregating Formula Results

- Use the **Calculation for Task and Group Summary Rows** option to aggregate data:
  - Sum: Adds up values for group or summary tasks.

○ Average: Calculates the mean for grouped tasks.

---

6. Displaying and Analyzing Formula Results

6.1 Adding Custom Fields to Views

- Insert the custom field as a column in the **Gantt Chart** or **Task Sheet** view.
- Format the column header for clarity (e.g., "Custom Risk Score").

6.2 Visualizing Data

- Use conditional formatting to highlight specific values.
  - ○ Example: Color-code tasks based on risk levels.

---

7. Advanced Techniques

7.1 Combining Multiple Conditions

- Use nested **IIf** statements for complex logic.
  - ○ Example: Multi-tier risk evaluation:
    ```
    IIf([Duration] > 15, "Critical", IIf([Duration] > 10, "High", "Low"))
    ```
  - ○ Copy

7.2 Linking to External Fields

- Create dependencies by referencing fields across tasks or resources.
  - ○ Example: Task priority based on resource availability:
    ```
    IIf([Resource Names] = "John Doe", "High", "Low")
    ```
  - ○ Copy

7.3 Dynamic Calculations

- Use formulas to track evolving metrics like earned value or schedule variance.

---

8. Troubleshooting Formulas

8.1 Common Errors

- **Syntax Errors**: Ensure proper use of brackets and functions.
- **Null Values**: Test for missing data using:
  ```
  IIf(IsNull([Field Name]), "N/A", [Field Name])
  ```
- Copy

8.2 Debugging Techniques

- Break down complex formulas into smaller parts.
- Test each component independently before combining them.

---

9. Best Practices

9.1 Keep Formulas Simple

- Use straightforward logic for clarity and maintainability.

9.2 Document Custom Formulas

- Record the purpose and structure of each formula for future reference.

9.3 Regularly Review and Update

- Periodically evaluate the relevance of your formulas and adjust them as project requirements change.

---

10. Summary

Leveraging formulas in Microsoft Project elevates your tracking and reporting capabilities. By automating calculations and creating custom metrics, you can gain deeper insights into your project performance and make data-driven decisions.

Key Takeaways:

- Formulas enable tailored tracking and analysis.
- Use logical, mathematical, and date functions for advanced customization.
- Test and refine formulas to ensure accuracy and relevance.

In the next chapter, we will explore **Using Macros to Automate Tasks**, diving into automating repetitive actions and enhancing productivity within Microsoft Project.

Using Macros to Automate Tasks

In Microsoft Project, macros are a powerful way to automate repetitive tasks, saving time and improving efficiency. This chapter will walk you through the process of creating, using, and managing macros within Microsoft Project. By the end of this chapter, you'll be able to streamline your workflow and reduce the manual effort involved in project management.

1. What Are Macros?

1.1 Defining Macros

- A **macro** is a series of commands or actions that are grouped together to perform a specific task automatically. Instead of executing each command individually, you can use a macro to execute them all at once, which saves time and minimizes errors.

1.2 Benefits of Using Macros

- **Efficiency**: Automate repetitive actions and tasks.
- **Consistency**: Ensure that the same steps are followed every time.
- **Error Reduction**: Reduce human errors that occur during repetitive tasks.

2. Setting Up Macros

2.1 Accessing the Macro Feature

- In Microsoft Project, macros are created and managed using the **Visual Basic for Applications (VBA)** editor.
- To access this, click on the **View** tab in the ribbon, then select **Macros** and click on **Visual Basic**.

2.2 Creating a New Macro

1. In the **VBA editor**, click on **Insert** and then **Module** to create a new module.
2. Write your macro using the **VBA** scripting language.
3. Example macro that marks all tasks as "Complete":

```
Sub MarkAllTasksComplete()
    Dim task As Task
    For Each task In ActiveProject.Tasks
        task.Status = "Complete"
    Next task
End Sub
```

- This script loops through all tasks in the project and sets their status to "Complete."

2.3 Assigning a Shortcut Key to the Macro

- You can assign a shortcut key to your macro for quick access:
    1. Go to **View > Macros > Macros**.
    2. Select the macro you want to assign a shortcut to, then click **Options**.
    3. In the **Macro Options** dialog, assign a shortcut key and click **OK**.

3. Managing and Editing Macros

3.1 Viewing Existing Macros

- To view and manage all macros in your project:
    1. Go to **View** > **Macros** > **Macros**.
    2. This will show a list of all available macros in your project.

3.2 Editing a Macro

- To edit a macro:
    1. Go to **View** > **Macros** > **Visual Basic**.
    2. In the **VBA editor**, select the macro you want to edit from the left pane.
    3. Modify the code as needed and press **F5** to run it.

---

4. Common Use Cases for Macros

4.1 Automating Task Updates

- Example: Automatically update task status based on completion percentage:

```
Sub UpdateTaskStatus()
    Dim task As Task
    For Each task In ActiveProject.Tasks
        If task.PercentComplete = 100 Then
            task.Status = "Complete"
        ElseIf task.PercentComplete > 0 Then
            task.Status = "In Progress"
        Else
            task.Status = "Not Started"
        End If
    Next task
End Sub
```

  - This macro loops through tasks and updates their status based on the completion percentage.

4.2 Scheduling Recurring Tasks

- Example: Automate the creation of recurring tasks such as weekly meetings:

```
Sub CreateRecurringTask()
    Dim newTask As Task
    Set newTask = ActiveProject.Tasks.Add("Weekly Meeting")
    newTask.Start = "1/1/2025"
    newTask.Duration = "1d"
    newTask.Recurring = True
    newTask.RecurringPattern = "Weekly"
End Sub
```

  - This macro creates a task named "Weekly Meeting" and sets it as a recurring task every week.

4.3 Formatting Project Views

- Example: Automatically apply a specific Gantt chart style:

```
Sub ApplyGanttStyle()
    ActiveProject.Application.ActiveGanttChartBarStyle.Text = "Task Name"
    ActiveProject.Application.ActiveGanttChartBarStyle.Color = RGB(0, 0,
255)
End Sub
```

  - This macro applies a specific style to all Gantt chart bars, changing the text and color.

---

5. Running and Testing Macros

5.1 Running a Macro

- To run a macro manually:
    1. Go to **View** > **Macros** > **Run Macro**.
    2. Select the macro you wish to run from the list.
    3. Click **Run**.

5.2 Debugging a Macro

- If the macro doesn't work as expected, use the **VBA editor**'s debugging tools:
    1. Set breakpoints to stop the code at specific lines.
    2. Use the **Immediate Window** to inspect variables and outputs.

---

6. Best Practices for Using Macros

6.1 Keep Macros Simple

- Focus on automating a single task or process at a time. Avoid overly complex macros, as they can become difficult to troubleshoot.

6.2 Save Your Macros

- Ensure your macros are saved as part of your project template so you can reuse them in future projects.

6.3 Document Your Macros

- Provide comments in your macro code to explain what each section does, making it easier to modify later or for other users to understand.

6.4 Test Thoroughly

- Test your macros on a sample project before running them on a live project. This will help catch any potential issues early.

---

7. Conclusion

Macros in Microsoft Project are an indispensable tool for automating tasks and increasing efficiency. They allow you to streamline repetitive activities, ensure consistency across your projects, and focus more on the strategic aspects of project management. By creating custom macros, you can tailor Microsoft Project to suit your unique workflow and maximize productivity.

Key Takeaways:

- Macros automate repetitive tasks and actions in Microsoft Project.
- Use **VBA** scripting to write custom macros.
- Keep macros simple, document them, and thoroughly test them before use.

In the next chapter, we will dive into **Maintaining Data Integrity** by ensuring that your project data remains accurate and consistent across the board.

Maintaining Data Integrity

Maintaining data integrity is one of the most critical aspects of managing a project in Microsoft Project. Accurate, reliable data ensures that project decisions are well-informed and that the project stays on track. This chapter explores strategies, tools, and best practices for maintaining data integrity, enabling you to manage your projects with confidence and precision.

1. Why Data Integrity Matters

1.1 Defining Data Integrity

Data integrity refers to the accuracy, consistency, and reliability of data throughout its lifecycle. In project management, this means ensuring that all tasks, resources, schedules, and financial data are accurate and up-to-date.

1.2 The Impact of Poor Data Integrity

- **Faulty Decision-Making**: Incorrect data leads to misguided project decisions.
- **Project Delays**: Inconsistent information can disrupt schedules and deadlines.
- **Resource Misallocation**: Poor data integrity can result in overuse or underuse of resources.
- **Eroded Stakeholder Confidence**: Inaccurate reports can reduce stakeholder trust in project management.

2. Strategies for Maintaining Data Integrity

2.1 Establishing a Single Source of Truth

- Use Microsoft Project as the central repository for all project-related data.
- Ensure that team members update the system regularly to avoid discrepancies between tools or documents.

2.2 Implementing Access Controls

- Restrict access to critical project files to authorized personnel.
- Assign roles and permissions to team members to prevent accidental modifications or deletions.

2.3 Regular Data Audits

- Schedule periodic checks to review project data for accuracy and completeness.
- Use built-in views, reports, and filters to identify missing or inconsistent data.

2.4 Version Control

- Maintain version histories of project files to track changes and revert to earlier versions if necessary.
- Enable Microsoft Project's backup and recovery features to safeguard data.

3. Tools in Microsoft Project to Support Data Integrity

3.1 Constraints and Dependencies

- Use task constraints and dependencies to enforce logical relationships between tasks.
- Set up task predecessors and successors to prevent scheduling conflicts.

3.2 Baselines

- Use baselines to capture the original project plan and compare it against actual progress.
- Regularly update and review baseline data to monitor project deviations.

3.3 Custom Fields

- Create and configure custom fields to capture additional data specific to your project needs.
- Use data validation rules in custom fields to ensure consistency and prevent invalid entries.

3.4 Resource Management Tools

- Allocate resources accurately using the **Resource Sheet** and **Resource Usage** views.
- Monitor resource availability and workload to avoid overallocation.

---

4. Preventing Data Errors

4.1 Setting Data Entry Standards

- Establish standard formats for data entry, such as date formats, task names, and resource identifiers.
- Train team members on these standards to minimize errors.

4.2 Automating Repetitive Tasks

- Use macros to automate data entry and updates, reducing the risk of human error.
- Example macro for checking empty fields:

```
Sub CheckEmptyFields()
    Dim task As Task
    For Each task In ActiveProject.Tasks
        If task.Text1 = "" Then
            MsgBox "Task " & task.Name & " has an empty custom field."
        End If
    Next task
End Sub
```

4.3 Validating Data

- Use filters and groupings to identify and correct anomalies, such as tasks without assigned resources or durations.
- Set up warnings or notifications for missing critical data fields.

---

5. Reviewing and Updating Data

5.1 Periodic Reviews

- Conduct regular review sessions with the project team to verify data accuracy.
- Use the **Task Inspector** to identify and resolve scheduling conflicts.

5.2 Using Reports for Verification

- Generate progress and variance reports to review discrepancies between planned and actual performance.
- Example reports:
  - **Task Variance Report**: Identifies tasks that are behind or ahead of schedule.
  - **Resource Work Report**: Highlights resource usage discrepancies.

5.3 Synchronizing with External Data Sources

- For projects integrated with tools like SharePoint or Project Online, ensure regular synchronization to avoid data mismatches.

---

6. Addressing Data Integrity Issues

6.1 Troubleshooting Data Discrepancies

- Use the **Task Usage** and **Resource Usage** views to identify and resolve inconsistencies in work or allocation data.
- Leverage the **Change Highlighting** feature to visualize the impact of data changes.

6.2 Correcting Errors

- Revisit historical data to identify patterns of errors or recurring issues.
- Educate team members on the root causes of errors and best practices to avoid them.

---

7. Best Practices for Maintaining Data Integrity

7.1 Keep Data Simple

- Avoid unnecessary complexity in your project data. Simpler data structures are easier to manage and less prone to errors.

7.2 Document Changes

- Maintain a log of changes made to the project plan, including the reasons for these changes.

7.3 Use Templates

- Create project templates with pre-configured settings and fields to ensure consistency across projects.

7.4 Foster Collaboration

- Involve the entire project team in maintaining data integrity. Encourage proactive communication and updates.

---

8. Conclusion

Maintaining data integrity is essential for successful project management. By leveraging Microsoft Project's tools and adhering to best practices, you can ensure your project data remains accurate, consistent, and reliable. This foundation of integrity empowers you to make informed decisions, stay on schedule, and build trust with stakeholders.

Key Takeaways:

- Use Microsoft Project as a centralized system for project data.
- Implement access controls, data validation, and automation to minimize errors.
- Regularly review and update project data to maintain its accuracy and relevance.

In the next chapter, we will explore how to finalize and document project deliverables to ensure a smooth project closure process.

Section XII:
Project Closure and Lessons Learned

Finalizing Deliverables and Documentation

As your project nears completion, ensuring that deliverables are finalized and documentation is complete is crucial for a successful project closure. This chapter focuses on the essential steps involved in finalizing deliverables, preparing project documentation, and ensuring all requirements have been met.

1. Importance of Finalizing Deliverables

1.1 Meeting Project Objectives

Finalizing deliverables ensures that all project goals and objectives have been achieved. This step confirms that the output aligns with the project scope and stakeholders' expectations.

1.2 Establishing Accountability

A formal review and acceptance process ensures accountability and prevents future disputes regarding the project outcomes.

1.3 Supporting Future Projects

Comprehensive documentation and finalized deliverables serve as valuable references for future projects, reducing redundancy and improving efficiency.

2. Steps to Finalize Deliverables

2.1 Review Deliverables Against Project Scope

- Compare deliverables with the initial project scope to ensure all requirements have been met.
- Use tools such as the **Deliverables Register** in Microsoft Project to track completion.

2.2 Conduct Quality Assurance

- Perform quality checks to ensure deliverables meet predefined standards.
- Use the **Task Inspector** in Microsoft Project to review task completions and ensure no discrepancies exist.

2.3 Stakeholder Acceptance

- Present deliverables to stakeholders for approval.
- Use the **Milestone Completion Report** or create a custom report to provide stakeholders with an overview of completed tasks.

2.4 Address Outstanding Issues

- Resolve any issues or discrepancies identified during the review and quality assurance processes.

- Record issue resolutions in the **Notes** section of tasks for future reference.

---

3. Preparing Project Documentation

3.1 Types of Documentation

- **Final Project Plan**: An updated version of the original project plan with all changes tracked.
- **Lessons Learned Document**: Highlights challenges faced, solutions implemented, and recommendations for future projects.
- **User Manuals and Guides**: For projects involving systems or software, provide user documentation.

3.2 Using Microsoft Project for Documentation

- Export project data into formats such as PDF or Excel for distribution.
- Use **Custom Reports** to generate tailored summaries, including schedules, budgets, and resource usage.

3.3 Version Control

- Maintain a version history of documents to track changes.
- Use Microsoft Project's **Save As** feature to preserve finalized versions with clear version naming conventions.

---

4. Tools in Microsoft Project for Deliverables and Documentation

4.1 Baselines

- Use baselines to capture the original plan and compare it against actual performance.
- Generate a **Variance Report** to highlight deviations and justify changes.

4.2 Reporting Tools

- **Built-In Reports**: Use reports such as **Project Overview** and **Cost Overview** to summarize key project outcomes.
- **Custom Dashboards**: Create dashboards to present data visually for stakeholders.

4.3 File Sharing and Integration

- Utilize integration with Microsoft 365 for seamless sharing of finalized documents.
- Synchronize with SharePoint or Project Online for centralized storage and team access.

---

5. Ensuring Deliverables Align with Stakeholder Expectations

5.1 Regular Stakeholder Communication

- Maintain regular updates with stakeholders throughout the project to ensure expectations are aligned.
- Use tools like the **Timeline View** to present progress in a clear, visual format.

5.2 Formal Handover Process

- Schedule a formal meeting or presentation to hand over deliverables.

- Document stakeholder feedback and approvals using Microsoft Project's **Task Notes** or integrated collaboration tools.

---

6. Archiving Deliverables and Documentation

6.1 Organizing Project Files

- Create a structured folder system for project files, separating deliverables, documentation, and reports.
- Use consistent naming conventions to facilitate easy retrieval.

6.2 Archiving in Microsoft Project

- Save the final project file in a secure location.
- Export key data to external formats for non-technical stakeholders.

6.3 Storing Lessons Learned

- Record lessons learned in a central repository for organizational knowledge.
- Use a custom **Lessons Learned Report** to summarize key insights and share them with the team.

---

7. Best Practices for Finalizing Deliverables and Documentation

7.1 Start Early

- Begin preparing documentation well before the project ends to avoid last-minute pressure.

7.2 Engage Stakeholders

- Actively involve stakeholders in the review and acceptance process to minimize misunderstandings.

7.3 Use Automation

- Leverage Microsoft Project's automation features to streamline reporting and documentation tasks.

7.4 Maintain Accuracy

- Double-check all documentation for accuracy and completeness before finalizing.

Conclusion: Finalizing deliverables and preparing comprehensive documentation are key steps in closing a project successfully. By leveraging Microsoft Project's tools and adhering to best practices, you can ensure that your project outcomes are delivered to satisfaction and future projects benefit from the knowledge gained.

Key Takeaways:

- Review deliverables against the project scope and perform quality checks.
- Use Microsoft Project to generate reports and export documentation.
- Organize and archive deliverables for future reference and knowledge sharing.

The next chapter will guide you through conducting a post-project review, where you'll analyze the project's success and areas for improvement.

Conducting Post-Project Review

A post-project review is a critical step in the project management lifecycle. It enables teams to evaluate what went well, what could have been improved, and how future projects can benefit from these insights. This chapter outlines the process of conducting a thorough post-project review and how Microsoft Project can facilitate this essential phase of project closure.

1. Understanding the Post-Project Review

1.1 Definition

A post-project review is a formal assessment conducted after project completion to evaluate the project's performance, processes, and outcomes. The goal is to capture lessons learned and identify actionable improvements for future projects.

1.2 Importance of Post-Project Reviews

- **Improves Organizational Learning:** Captures insights that can enhance future project performance.
- **Enhances Team Development:** Provides constructive feedback to improve skills and collaboration.
- **Validates Successes:** Recognizes accomplishments and builds morale.

2. Preparing for the Post-Project Review

2.1 Assemble the Review Team

- Include key stakeholders, project team members, and, if applicable, external consultants.
- Ensure representation from all functional areas involved in the project.

2.2 Gather Project Data

- Export project metrics and reports from Microsoft Project, such as task performance, resource utilization, and budget tracking.
- Collect feedback from stakeholders and team members using surveys or structured interviews.

2.3 Schedule the Review Meeting

- Allocate sufficient time for an in-depth discussion.
- Share relevant project data and reports with participants in advance.

3. Steps in Conducting the Post-Project Review

3.1 Review Project Objectives

- Revisit the initial project goals and scope.
- Compare the planned deliverables with the actual outcomes using Microsoft Project's **Baseline Reports**.

3.2 Analyze Performance Metrics

- **Time:** Evaluate whether tasks were completed within the scheduled timelines.
- **Budget:** Assess budget adherence using Microsoft Project's **Cost Overview Report**.
- **Quality:** Review quality benchmarks and client feedback.

3.3 Identify Successes

- Highlight milestones achieved on time or ahead of schedule.
- Recognize high-performing team members and successful strategies.

3.4 Discuss Challenges and Lessons Learned

- Identify key challenges faced during the project, such as resource constraints or delays.
- Document lessons learned using Microsoft Project's **Notes** feature or by creating a custom **Lessons Learned Report**.

3.5 Develop Actionable Recommendations

- Recommend process improvements or tools that could enhance future projects.
- Identify training needs or areas for skill development within the team.

---

4. Tools in Microsoft Project for Post-Project Review

4.1 Variance Reports

- Use variance analysis to compare actual performance against the baseline.
- Generate the **Task Variance Report** to identify discrepancies in task durations and dependencies.

4.2 Resource Utilization Reports

- Analyze how effectively resources were allocated and utilized during the project.
- Use the **Resource Overview Report** to pinpoint overallocations or underutilizations.

4.3 Customized Dashboards

- Create dashboards that consolidate key metrics such as cost, progress, and resource usage.
- Share these dashboards with stakeholders for easy visualization of project outcomes.

---

5. Best Practices for an Effective Review

5.1 Foster an Open Environment

- Encourage honest and constructive feedback.
- Emphasize that the review is a learning opportunity rather than a fault-finding exercise.

5.2 Focus on Data-Driven Insights

- Base discussions on factual data from Microsoft Project reports and stakeholder feedback.
- Avoid subjective judgments and assumptions.

5.3 Document and Share Findings

- Summarize the review's outcomes in a formal report.
- Distribute the findings to relevant stakeholders and archive the document for future reference.

5.4 Create a Follow-Up Plan

- Assign action items to team members based on the recommendations from the review.
- Use Microsoft Project's **Task Assignment** feature to track follow-up activities.

6. Example of a Post-Project Review Agenda

Time	Activity	Description
10:00 - 10:15	Opening Remarks	Welcome and outline the review objectives.
10:15 - 10:45	Project Metrics Overview	Present data on time, cost, and quality.
10:45 - 11:15	Successes and Challenges Discussion	Identify strengths and areas for improvement.
11:15 - 11:45	Lessons Learned and Recommendations	Develop actionable insights and strategies.
11:45 - 12:00	Closing and Next Steps	Summarize findings and assign action items.

7. Leveraging Lessons Learned for Future Projects

7.1 Creating a Lessons Learned Repository

- Consolidate all lessons learned into a centralized repository accessible to future project teams.
- Use Microsoft Project's **Shared Workspace** or integrate with tools like SharePoint.

7.2 Applying Insights

- Incorporate insights into project templates and workflows.
- Update standard operating procedures (SOPs) to reflect improved practices.

8. Conclusion

Conducting a thorough post-project review is an invaluable practice for continuous improvement in project management. By leveraging Microsoft Project's robust tools, you can ensure a structured, data-driven review process that benefits both current and future projects.

Key Takeaways:

- Assemble the right team and prepare comprehensive project data.
- Focus on successes, challenges, and actionable lessons learned.
- Use Microsoft Project to generate insights and share findings effectively.

The next chapter will guide you through capturing the lessons learned and archiving reusable project templates for streamlined project planning.

Capturing Lessons Learned for Future Projects

Capturing lessons learned is a critical component of project closure. This process not only facilitates continuous improvement but also ensures that both successes and challenges contribute to organizational growth. In this chapter, we explore the importance of documenting lessons learned, the steps to capture them effectively, and how to use Microsoft Project and associated tools to streamline the process.

1. Understanding the Value of Lessons Learned

1.1 Definition

Lessons learned are insights gained throughout the lifecycle of a project. They encompass both positive experiences that should be repeated and negative outcomes that should be avoided.

1.2 Importance

- **Continuous Improvement:** Enhances processes for future projects.
- **Cost and Time Efficiency:** Prevents repeated mistakes, saving resources.
- **Knowledge Sharing:** Builds a repository of insights accessible to the entire organization.

2. The Lessons Learned Process

2.1 Timing

Capture lessons learned during and after the project. Ongoing documentation ensures that real-time insights are not forgotten, while post-project reviews provide a comprehensive perspective.

2.2 Participants

Involve key stakeholders, project team members, and, if applicable, external consultants to ensure diverse viewpoints.

2.3 Structured Approach

Organize lessons learned into categories such as:

- **Processes:** What workflows succeeded or failed?
- **Resources:** Were allocations effective?
- **Timeline:** Were deadlines realistic?
- **Communication:** Was stakeholder engagement effective?

3. Steps to Capture Lessons Learned

3.1 Conduct a Review Meeting

Organize a meeting with project stakeholders to discuss experiences. Use structured agendas to facilitate focused discussions.

3.2 Collect Data

Gather quantitative and qualitative data using:

- **Microsoft Project Reports:** Extract insights on task progress, resource utilization, and variances.
- **Surveys and Feedback Forms:** Solicit input from team members and stakeholders.

3.3 Document Insights

Record lessons learned in a standardized format to ensure clarity and accessibility. Use Microsoft Project's **Notes** feature or integrate with tools like SharePoint or OneNote.

---

4. Leveraging Microsoft Project for Lessons Learned

4.1 Reports

- **Variance Reports:** Analyze deviations from baseline plans to identify areas for improvement.
- **Resource Usage Reports:** Evaluate resource allocation and identify bottlenecks.

4.2 Custom Fields

Create custom fields to capture lessons learned directly within the project file. For example:

- Add a field for "Lesson Type" (e.g., success, challenge).
- Add a "Recommendation" field to document actionable steps.

4.3 Visual Dashboards

Use dashboards to present summarized lessons learned for easy review by stakeholders.

4.4 Shared Templates

Incorporate lessons learned into project templates to embed improvements into future workflows.

---

5. Best Practices for Capturing Lessons Learned

5.1 Foster Transparency

Encourage open discussions where team members feel safe sharing their experiences, both positive and negative.

5.2 Focus on Solutions

Rather than dwelling on failures, emphasize actionable steps to improve future projects.

5.3 Prioritize Key Insights

While capturing all insights is ideal, focus on those that have the highest potential impact on future projects.

---

6. Documenting Lessons Learned

6.1 Standardized Format

Use a consistent format to ensure clarity and accessibility. A typical template includes:

- **Project Name**
- **Objective**

- **Key Successes**
- **Challenges**
- **Recommendations**
- **Responsible Party for Follow-Up**

6.2 Central Repository

Store lessons learned in a centralized repository, such as a SharePoint site or Microsoft Teams workspace, for easy access by future project teams.

---

7. Applying Lessons Learned

7.1 Update Project Management Templates

Incorporate actionable insights into project templates and workflows.

7.2 Conduct Training

Train team members on best practices and lessons learned to build organizational capacity.

7.3 Monitor Application

Ensure that insights are applied effectively in future projects by tracking implementation.

---

8. Example: Lessons Learned Documentation

Category	Lesson	Recommendation	Owner
Timeline	Deadlines were missed due to insufficient task buffers.	Add buffer time for critical tasks in future plans.	Project Manager
Resource Allocation	Team members were overallocated during peak phases.	Improve resource leveling in project scheduling.	Resource Planner
Communication	Stakeholder updates were delayed.	Schedule bi-weekly update meetings in the plan.	Communications Lead

---

Conclusion: Capturing lessons learned ensures that every project contributes to the organization's growth and efficiency. By leveraging Microsoft Project's features, teams can standardize, document, and apply insights to enhance future project outcomes.

Key Takeaways:

- Schedule regular reviews to capture lessons throughout the project.
- Use Microsoft Project tools to document and analyze insights.
- Apply lessons learned to templates, workflows, and team training.

The next chapter will explore how to archive completed projects and reuse templates effectively, ensuring a seamless transition from closure to new project planning.

Archiving and Reusing Project Templates

Effectively closing out a project involves more than just delivering the final product. It includes proper documentation, archiving, and the preparation of reusable templates for future projects. In this chapter, we'll explore the significance of archiving project data, how to create and manage project templates in Microsoft Project, and best practices for ensuring these templates remain relevant and accessible.

1. The Importance of Archiving and Templates

1.1 Why Archive Projects?

- **Historical Reference:** Archived projects provide a record of decisions, changes, and milestones.
- **Audit Compliance:** Retain data for regulatory or contractual obligations.
- **Lessons Learned:** Preserve key insights for future application.

1.2 Benefits of Reusable Templates

- **Efficiency:** Reduce setup time for similar projects.
- **Consistency:** Standardize project planning and execution across the organization.
- **Quality Assurance:** Incorporate best practices and proven strategies into every project.

2. Archiving Projects in Microsoft Project

2.1 Preparing a Project for Archiving

Before archiving, ensure the following steps are completed:

1. **Finalize the Project:** Confirm all tasks are marked as completed, and the project is saved with the final status.
2. **Update Baselines and Reports:** Save any final baselines or generate reports for future reference.
3. **Resolve Overallocations:** Ensure resource leveling issues are addressed to provide an accurate historical record.

2.2 Saving an Archived Project

Microsoft Project provides several ways to save project data:

- **File Formats:**
  - Save the project in **.MPP** format for ongoing compatibility.
  - Export as a **PDF** or **Excel** file for sharing and easy reference.
- **Cloud Storage:**
  - Use platforms like **OneDrive** or **SharePoint** to store archived projects in a central repository.
- **Version Control:**
  - Implement a naming convention (e.g., "ProjectName_Year_Final") to differentiate archived files.

2.3 Securing Archived Data

- **Access Permissions:** Restrict access to sensitive project data to authorized personnel.
- **Backups:** Regularly back up archived files to prevent data loss.
- **Metadata:** Include key project information (e.g., project manager, completion date, client name) for easy identification.

3. Creating Reusable Project Templates

3.1 What to Include in a Template

A good project template should incorporate:

- **Standardized Tasks:** Include common phases such as initiation, planning, execution, and closure.
- **Resource Assignments:** Pre-define frequently used resources for quick allocation.
- **Calendars and Work Schedules:** Set default working hours and holidays.
- **Custom Fields:** Include fields for tracking specific metrics like risks or budget categories.
- **Pre-Linked Dependencies:** Define task relationships to streamline scheduling.

3.2 Steps to Create a Template

1. **Start from a Completed Project:** Use a successful project as a baseline for the template.
2. **Remove Project-Specific Data:** Delete unique tasks, dates, or assignments that won't apply to other projects.
3. **Save as a Template:**
   - Navigate to **File > Save As** and select **Project Template (*.MPT)** as the format.
   - Provide a clear name (e.g., "WebsiteDevelopmentTemplate").

3.3 Managing Templates

- **Central Repository:** Store templates in a shared location like **Project Online**, **SharePoint**, or a network drive.
- **Version Updates:** Regularly review templates to incorporate new lessons learned or process changes.
- **Naming Standards:** Use consistent naming conventions to help users identify the right template quickly.

---

4. Using Project Templates

4.1 Starting a New Project from a Template

1. Open Microsoft Project.
2. Navigate to **File > New** and select the desired template.
3. Customize the template by adding project-specific details such as start dates, team members, and deliverables.

4.2 Modifying Existing Templates

- Adjust tasks, dependencies, or resource assignments to fit the unique requirements of a new project.
- Save the modified version as a new file to preserve the original template.

4.3 Scaling Templates for Different Project Sizes

For larger or more complex projects, break down templates into smaller, manageable sections. For instance:

- Use separate templates for different phases, such as "Planning Phase Template" or "Execution Phase Template."
- Combine multiple templates into a master project plan if needed.

5. Best Practices for Archiving and Templates

5.1 Archiving

- **Document Everything:** Include meeting notes, change requests, and final reports.
- **Tag and Categorize:** Assign tags (e.g., industry type, project size) to make archived projects easier to locate.
- **Review Annually:** Audit archived files to ensure data integrity and relevance.

5.2 Templates

- **Avoid Overloading:** Keep templates streamlined by including only essential elements.
- **Involve Stakeholders:** Gather input from team members to create templates that reflect actual needs.
- **Train Users:** Provide training on how to use and modify templates effectively.

6. Example: Archiving and Template Workflow

1. **Complete the Project:**
   - Mark all tasks as complete and update the project file.
2. **Save Final Reports:**
   - Generate a cost overview and a schedule variance report.
3. **Archive the Project:**
   - Save the project file in a shared folder named "2025 Completed Projects."
4. **Create a Template:**
   - Remove specific client details and save the file as "ITImplementationTemplate."
5. **Apply the Template:**
   - Use the new template for a similar upcoming IT project, customizing it as needed.

7. Conclusion

Archiving and reusing project templates are essential for efficient and effective project management. By properly storing past projects and leveraging templates, you can save time, improve consistency, and continuously refine your processes. Microsoft Project offers robust features to support these efforts, ensuring that every project builds on the foundation of past successes.

Key Takeaways:

- Archive projects with detailed documentation for future reference.
- Create templates that reflect best practices and streamline planning.
- Regularly update and review templates to ensure they remain relevant and effective.

The next chapter will focus on staying current with Microsoft Project updates, enabling teams to adapt to evolving tools and methodologies effectively.

Section XIII:
Evolving with Microsoft Project

Staying Current with Updates and New Features

Microsoft Project is a dynamic tool that evolves regularly to meet the demands of modern project management. Staying updated with the latest features and enhancements ensures you can fully leverage its capabilities for efficient project planning and execution. In this chapter, we'll explore strategies for staying informed about updates, an overview of recent features, and tips for integrating new functionalities into your workflows.

---

1. Importance of Staying Current

1.1 Benefits of Regular Updates

- **Improved Efficiency:** Access to new tools and features that streamline project management processes.
- **Enhanced Collaboration:** Better integration with other Microsoft 365 tools and services.
- **Security and Stability:** Latest updates often include critical security patches and performance improvements.
- **Competitive Edge:** Stay ahead of industry standards by utilizing the latest project management capabilities.

1.2 Risks of Falling Behind

- **Obsolete Features:** Older versions may lack compatibility with updated software and tools.
- **Security Vulnerabilities:** Older versions are more prone to cyber threats.
- **Lost Productivity:** Missing out on new features that could improve efficiency.

---

2. Understanding Microsoft's Update Cycles

2.1 Types of Updates

Microsoft Project updates can be categorized into:

- **Feature Updates:** Introduce new capabilities, tools, or interface improvements.
- **Security Updates:** Address vulnerabilities to protect against threats.
- **Bug Fixes:** Resolve known issues or glitches in the software.

2.2 Update Channels

Microsoft offers different update channels based on user needs:

- **Current Channel:** Provides the latest updates as soon as they are released. Ideal for users who want immediate access to new features.
- **Monthly Enterprise Channel:** Updates less frequently but ensures stability and reliability for enterprise users.

- **Semi-Annual Enterprise Channel:** Updates every six months, providing a balance of new features and tested reliability.

---

3. Staying Informed About Updates

3.1 Official Microsoft Sources

- **Microsoft 365 Admin Center:** View release notes, updates, and upcoming changes.
- **Microsoft Project Blog:** Regularly updated with feature announcements, best practices, and tips.
- **Release Notes:** Access detailed information about updates on Microsoft's official website.

3.2 Community Resources

- **User Forums:** Engage with other Microsoft Project users to discuss updates and share experiences.
- **LinkedIn Groups:** Join project management groups to stay informed about industry trends and software updates.
- **Conferences and Webinars:** Attend events hosted by Microsoft or other organizations to learn about the latest tools.

3.3 Automatic Notifications

- Enable update notifications in Microsoft Project to receive alerts when new features are available.
- Subscribe to Microsoft's email newsletters or RSS feeds for the latest news.

---

4. Recent Features in Microsoft Project

Microsoft regularly enhances Project with innovative features. Here are some recent highlights:

- **Roadmap Integration:** Create high-level project roadmaps that align with organizational goals.
- **Agile Management Tools:** Support for Kanban boards and Scrum methodologies.
- **Enhanced Collaboration:** Better integration with Microsoft Teams and Planner for real-time updates and communication.
- **AI-Powered Insights:** Leverage artificial intelligence to predict project outcomes and recommend optimizations.
- **Custom Reporting Improvements:** Advanced options for building custom dashboards and reports.

---

5. Integrating New Features into Your Workflow

5.1 Exploring New Features

- **Hands-On Practice:** Use a test project to experiment with new tools and functionalities.
- **Training Resources:** Utilize Microsoft's training guides, videos, and tutorials to understand new features.
- **Team Workshops:** Organize team sessions to familiarize everyone with updated capabilities.

5.2 Updating Processes

- **Analyze Impact:** Evaluate how a new feature aligns with your project management processes.
- **Implement Gradually:** Introduce new features in phases to avoid overwhelming the team.

- **Feedback Loop:** Encourage team members to provide feedback on how new features enhance or hinder their workflows.

---

6. Automating Updates

6.1 Enabling Automatic Updates

- Open Microsoft Project.
- Go to **File > Account > Update Options** and select **Enable Updates.**
- This ensures your software is always up-to-date without manual intervention.

6.2 Scheduling Updates

- For teams using shared devices, schedule updates during off-peak hours to minimize disruptions.
- Notify team members in advance of any significant updates that may impact workflows.

---

7. Addressing Update Challenges

7.1 Common Challenges

- **Compatibility Issues:** Older projects may face compatibility problems with new features.
- **Learning Curve:** Adapting to new tools can initially slow down productivity.
- **Resistance to Change:** Team members may be hesitant to adopt unfamiliar features.

7.2 Solutions

- **Backward Compatibility:** Test older files with new versions before widespread adoption.
- **Training Programs:** Offer training sessions and documentation to ease the transition.
- **Change Management:** Communicate the benefits of updates to gain team buy-in.

---

8. Planning for Future Updates

8.1 Proactive Monitoring

- Regularly check Microsoft's roadmap for upcoming updates to plan accordingly.
- Align update schedules with organizational milestones to avoid disruptions.

8.2 Continuous Learning

- Designate a team member as a Microsoft Project champion to stay informed and train others.
- Encourage team members to attend training sessions or webinars on new features.

---

9. Example: Adopting Agile Features

Scenario: Your organization wants to incorporate Agile methodologies into its projects.

1. **Learn the Feature:** Explore Microsoft Project's Kanban boards and sprint planning tools.
2. **Pilot Program:** Implement Agile features in a smaller project to test their effectiveness.
3. **Team Training:** Conduct a workshop to train team members on using Agile tools.

4. **Evaluate and Expand:** Gather feedback from the pilot and roll out the features across other projects.

---

10. Conclusion

Staying current with updates and new features in Microsoft Project is critical for maintaining efficiency, security, and competitiveness in project management. By proactively monitoring updates, training your team, and integrating new tools into workflows, you can ensure your projects remain aligned with the latest industry standards.

Key Takeaways:

- Regular updates bring new tools, improved security, and better performance.
- Utilize Microsoft's resources and community support to stay informed about changes.
- Gradually integrate new features into your workflows with proper training and feedback.

The next chapter will focus on adapting to Agile and hybrid methodologies, providing insights on managing flexible and evolving project requirements.

Adapting to Agile and Hybrid Methodologies

As project management evolves, methodologies like Agile and hybrid approaches have become critical for managing projects in dynamic and flexible environments. Microsoft Project supports these methodologies with features tailored to Agile and hybrid workflows, enabling project managers to meet evolving requirements efficiently. This chapter explores how to adapt Microsoft Project to Agile and hybrid methodologies, including configuring settings, managing Agile workflows, and integrating traditional and Agile approaches in hybrid projects.

1. Understanding Agile and Hybrid Methodologies

1.1 Agile Methodology

Agile focuses on iterative development, incremental delivery, and continuous feedback. It is widely used in industries like software development, where requirements can evolve throughout the project lifecycle.

Key Principles:

- Collaboration and customer feedback.
- Iterative workflows with sprints.
- Emphasis on flexibility and adaptability.

1.2 Hybrid Methodology

Hybrid project management combines the structured approach of traditional methodologies (like Waterfall) with the flexibility of Agile. This approach allows teams to leverage the strengths of both methods, making it suitable for complex projects with varied requirements.

Key Features:

- Fixed deliverables with iterative processes.
- Coexistence of predictive and adaptive approaches.
- Integration of traditional milestones with Agile sprints.

2. Configuring Microsoft Project for Agile Workflows

2.1 Creating an Agile Project

Microsoft Project includes templates for Scrum and Kanban methodologies. To create an Agile project:

1. **Open Microsoft Project.**
2. Go to **File > New.**
3. Select an **Agile template** (Scrum or Kanban) to configure the workspace.

2.2 Agile Boards and Views

Microsoft Project offers Agile boards for managing tasks visually:

- **Kanban Board:** Ideal for workflows focused on task progress (e.g., To Do, In Progress, Done).
- **Sprint Board:** Suited for Scrum teams working in iterative sprints.

To access Agile views:

- Select the **View tab** in the Ribbon.
- Choose **Task Board** or **Sprint Planning Board.**

2.3 Defining Sprints

Sprints are time-boxed iterations in Agile workflows. To define sprints in Microsoft Project:

1. Go to **Project > Agile > Manage Sprints.**
2. Specify the duration and start date for each sprint.
3. Assign tasks to specific sprints.

---

3. Managing Agile Projects in Microsoft Project

3.1 Adding Tasks

- Use the **Backlog View** to add and prioritize tasks.
- Drag and drop tasks into sprint buckets on the board.

3.2 Tracking Progress

- Mark tasks as **Completed** or move them between columns (e.g., In Progress, Testing).
- Use the **Task Board View** to monitor overall progress at a glance.

3.3 Generating Agile Reports

Microsoft Project offers reporting features for Agile workflows:

- **Burndown Charts:** Track the completion of work against the sprint timeline.
- **Velocity Reports:** Measure the team's capacity and delivery rate over sprints.

---

4. Implementing Hybrid Methodologies

4.1 Combining Waterfall and Agile

Hybrid projects often require integrating Waterfall milestones with Agile iterations:

1. Use traditional Gantt Chart views for tracking high-level milestones.
2. Incorporate Agile sprints or Kanban boards for iterative task management.

4.2 Linking Agile and Traditional Tasks

- Use task dependencies to link Agile tasks with traditional deliverables.
- Assign Agile tasks to specific milestones to create a unified timeline.

4.3 Managing Resources in Hybrid Projects

- Combine resource allocation for Agile teams and traditional tasks in the **Resource Sheet.**
- Monitor workloads to ensure balanced resource utilization across methodologies.

---

5. Benefits of Agile and Hybrid Methodologies in Microsoft Project

5.1 Agile Benefits

- Flexibility to respond to changes.
- Continuous delivery of value through iterative sprints.
- Enhanced collaboration with visual task boards.

5.2 Hybrid Benefits

- Balance between structure and flexibility.
- Improved stakeholder communication with milestones and sprints.
- Tailored workflows for complex project requirements.

---

6. Example: Transitioning to a Hybrid Methodology

Scenario: A software development team is integrating hardware components into their project, requiring a mix of Waterfall and Agile approaches.

Steps:

1. **Set Up the Project:**
   - Define hardware milestones using the Gantt Chart view.
   - Use the Scrum template for software development tasks.
2. **Define Dependencies:**
   - Link hardware milestones to sprint deliverables.
3. **Monitor Progress:**
   - Use the Sprint Planning Board for Agile tasks.
   - Track overall progress with the Gantt Chart.
4. **Adjust as Needed:**
   - Reallocate resources dynamically based on task progress.

---

7. Challenges and Solutions

7.1 Challenges

- **Learning Curve:** Team members may struggle to adapt to new workflows.
- **Integration Issues:** Combining methodologies can lead to misalignment.
- **Overlapping Workflows:** Managing parallel processes may increase complexity.

7.2 Solutions

- Provide training on Agile features in Microsoft Project.
- Use clear communication to align teams on hybrid workflows.
- Regularly review and adjust processes to ensure seamless integration.

---

8. Tips for Success

- **Start Small:** Pilot Agile or hybrid methodologies on smaller projects before full-scale implementation.
- **Leverage Templates:** Use Microsoft Project's predefined templates to save setup time.
- **Foster Collaboration:** Encourage cross-functional teams to communicate regularly.

---

9. Conclusion

Adapting to Agile and hybrid methodologies in Microsoft Project enables organizations to meet evolving project demands with flexibility and precision. By leveraging Microsoft Project's robust tools, teams can seamlessly transition between traditional and iterative workflows, ensuring successful project delivery.

Key Takeaways:

- Agile workflows enhance flexibility and responsiveness.
- Hybrid methodologies balance structured planning with adaptability.
- Microsoft Project provides versatile tools for managing Agile and hybrid projects.

The next chapter will focus on exploring add-ons and integrations to further enhance Microsoft Project's capabilities.

Exploring Add-Ons and Integrations

Microsoft Project is a powerful tool on its own, but its capabilities can be significantly enhanced through various add-ons and integrations. These tools provide extended functionality for collaboration, reporting, automation, and more, allowing teams to tailor the application to their unique project management needs. In this chapter, we'll explore popular add-ons, integrations with Microsoft and third-party tools, and best practices for leveraging these resources effectively.

1. The Role of Add-Ons and Integrations

1.1 Enhancing Core Capabilities

Add-ons and integrations can:

- Improve collaboration across teams and tools.
- Automate repetitive processes for greater efficiency.
- Provide advanced reporting and analytics capabilities.

1.2 Customizing Workflows

By integrating Microsoft Project with other tools, you can:

- Streamline communication.
- Enable seamless data sharing.
- Tailor workflows to specific organizational requirements.

2. Add-Ons to Extend Microsoft Project

2.1 Microsoft Project Add-Ins

Microsoft provides several official add-ins through the Office Store that enhance functionality within Project. Popular options include:

- **Task Scheduler Enhancements**: Tools for optimizing task scheduling and dependencies.
- **Advanced Reporting Templates**: Prebuilt templates for complex reporting needs.
- **Agile Board Enhancements**: Add-ons for Agile and hybrid workflows.

2.2 Third-Party Add-Ons

Third-party providers also offer specialized tools for Microsoft Project:

- **OnePager Pro**: For creating visually appealing timelines and Gantt charts.
- **Sensei Task Analyzer**: Analyzes task structure to identify potential issues.
- **Project Plan 365**: Extends compatibility and collaboration for non-Project users.

2.3 Installation and Setup

To install an add-on:

1. Open Microsoft Project.
2. Navigate to the **File > Options > Add-ins** menu.
3. Browse the Office Store or upload a custom add-in file.
4. Follow the on-screen instructions to complete installation.

3. Integrating Microsoft Project with Microsoft Tools

3.1 Microsoft Teams

Integrate Microsoft Project with Teams to improve collaboration:

- Add a Project tab in a Teams channel to share plans directly.
- Use Teams for real-time updates and discussions.
- Schedule and manage meetings tied to project timelines.

3.2 Microsoft Power BI

Power BI allows advanced reporting and data visualization:

- Import Microsoft Project data for dynamic dashboards.
- Use built-in templates for Gantt charts, timelines, and progress tracking.
- Automate report generation and distribution.

3.3 SharePoint and OneDrive

These integrations enhance file management:

- Store and access project files securely in SharePoint or OneDrive.
- Sync files for offline access and automatic updates.
- Enable version control for collaborative editing.

3.4 Power Automate

Automate workflows with Power Automate:

- Set up triggers for task updates, reminders, and approvals.
- Connect Project to other Microsoft applications for seamless data flow.

---

4. Integrating Microsoft Project with Third-Party Tools

4.1 Collaboration Tools

- **Slack**: Sync tasks and updates from Project to Slack channels for quick communication.
- **Asana or Trello**: Share task progress across tools to involve external collaborators.

4.2 CRM and ERP Systems

- **Salesforce**: Align project plans with customer management systems for consistent delivery.
- **SAP**: Sync resource and financial data for better forecasting and cost management.

4.3 Development Tools

- **Jira**: Combine Project's planning features with Jira's Agile boards for software development teams.
- **GitHub**: Track code changes and link them to project tasks.

4.4 Document Management

- **Google Workspace**: Share project data with Google Sheets, Docs, and Drive for broader accessibility.

5. Key Benefits of Add-Ons and Integrations

- **Improved Collaboration**: Centralize communication and task management across tools.
- **Enhanced Reporting**: Use advanced analytics for data-driven decisions.
- **Increased Productivity**: Reduce manual effort with automated workflows.
- **Customization**: Tailor Microsoft Project to meet specific project requirements.

6. Steps for Successful Integration

6.1 Define Objectives

Identify the goals of integrating add-ons or third-party tools. For example:

- Streamlining communication.
- Enhancing reporting capabilities.
- Automating repetitive tasks.

6.2 Evaluate Compatibility

Ensure that add-ons and integrations are compatible with your version of Microsoft Project and other tools in your tech stack.

6.3 Pilot the Integration

Test integrations on smaller projects to identify potential challenges before scaling up.

6.4 Train the Team

Provide training to ensure all users understand how to leverage the integrations effectively.

7. Example Use Case: Microsoft Project and Power BI

Scenario: A project manager needs detailed, real-time dashboards to present to stakeholders.

Solution:

1. Export Microsoft Project data to Power BI using the built-in connector.
2. Create interactive dashboards with task progress, resource allocation, and budget tracking.
3. Share reports via Power BI to ensure stakeholders have up-to-date insights.

8. Common Challenges and Solutions

8.1 Integration Complexity

Challenge: Setting up integrations can be time-consuming. **Solution:** Use templates and prebuilt connectors provided by Microsoft and trusted third-party providers.

8.2 Data Synchronization Issues

Challenge: Data discrepancies between tools. **Solution:** Schedule regular sync intervals and use error-checking mechanisms.

8.3 User Resistance

Challenge: Teams may resist new tools. **Solution:** Communicate the benefits clearly and provide hands-on training.

---

9. Tips for Optimizing Add-Ons and Integrations

- Regularly review add-on usage to ensure relevance and efficiency.
- Keep software and add-ons updated to avoid compatibility issues.
- Monitor integration performance and troubleshoot errors promptly.

---

10. Conclusion

Exploring add-ons and integrations unlocks the full potential of Microsoft Project, transforming it into a comprehensive project management ecosystem. Whether you're automating workflows, enhancing reporting, or improving collaboration, these tools allow for greater flexibility and efficiency.

Key Takeaways:

- Integrations with tools like Power BI and Teams enhance reporting and collaboration.
- Third-party add-ons extend the core functionality of Microsoft Project.
- Regular reviews and updates ensure seamless integration performance.

The next chapter will guide you through planning your ongoing learning path to stay proficient in Microsoft Project and project management best practices.

Planning Your Ongoing Learning Path

The field of project management and the tools supporting it, including Microsoft Project, are constantly evolving. Staying updated with new features, methodologies, and best practices is crucial for remaining effective and competitive in project management. This chapter provides actionable strategies for planning your ongoing learning path to ensure you consistently build your skills and adapt to changes in the software and the industry.

1. The Importance of Continuous Learning

1.1 Keeping Up with Software Updates

Microsoft Project frequently releases updates to enhance functionality, improve usability, and address security concerns. Staying current with these updates ensures:

- Access to new features and tools.
- Enhanced productivity and efficiency.
- Greater compatibility with other software.

1.2 Evolving Methodologies

Project management methodologies like Agile, Scrum, and hybrid approaches continue to gain traction. Understanding and adopting these methodologies can help you manage projects more effectively in dynamic environments.

1.3 Advancing Career Opportunities

Continuous learning positions you as a knowledgeable and adaptive professional, opening doors to advanced roles and certifications.

2. Creating a Learning Plan

2.1 Define Your Learning Objectives

Start by identifying your goals:

- Mastering advanced Microsoft Project features.
- Understanding new project management methodologies.
- Gaining certifications in project management.

2.2 Break Learning into Manageable Steps

Divide your learning objectives into smaller, actionable steps. For example:

1. Focus on mastering one feature or methodology at a time.
2. Set monthly or quarterly learning goals.

2.3 Allocate Time for Learning

Dedicate specific time slots for professional development. Even 30 minutes per week can add up significantly over time.

3. Leveraging Microsoft Learning Resources

3.1 Microsoft Learn

- **Description**: Microsoft's official learning platform offers free courses, documentation, and certifications for Microsoft Project.
- **Content**: Step-by-step tutorials, case studies, and best practices.
- **Access**: Visit Microsoft Learn.

3.2 Microsoft 365 Blog

- **Description**: A blog with the latest updates and tips for Microsoft Project and other 365 tools.
- **Content**: Announcements, feature highlights, and integration guides.

3.3 Webinars and Events

Microsoft frequently hosts live webinars and events. These sessions provide insights into the latest tools and offer opportunities to interact with experts.

---

4. Enrolling in Professional Training

4.1 Online Courses

- Platforms like **LinkedIn Learning**, **Udemy**, and **Coursera** offer in-depth courses on Microsoft Project and project management methodologies.
- Look for courses with hands-on exercises and real-world scenarios.

4.2 Certifications

Consider pursuing certifications such as:

- **Microsoft Certified: Project Manager Associate**: Focused on Microsoft Project.
- **PMP (Project Management Professional)**: Industry-standard certification.
- **Certified Scrum Master (CSM)**: Agile methodology certification.

4.3 In-Person Workshops

Local workshops and bootcamps provide immersive learning experiences and opportunities to network with other professionals.

---

5. Joining Professional Communities

5.1 Online Forums and Groups

Engage in communities like:

- **ProjectManagement.com**: Discussions, templates, and webinars.
- **Microsoft Project Forum**: A space for troubleshooting and sharing tips.

5.2 Social Media and Networking Platforms

- **LinkedIn Groups**: Join groups focused on Microsoft Project and project management.
- **Reddit**: Participate in relevant threads like r/ProjectManagement.

5.3 Local Meetups

Find meetups or user groups in your area for project managers and Microsoft Project users to exchange ideas and experiences.

---

6. Practicing What You Learn

6.1 Apply New Skills to Current Projects

Start small by incorporating new features or methodologies into your ongoing projects.

6.2 Create Practice Projects

Set up mock projects to test and refine your skills without the pressure of real-world deadlines.

6.3 Seek Feedback

Share your work with colleagues or mentors to get constructive feedback and identify areas for improvement.

---

7. Staying Motivated

7.1 Celebrate Milestones

Acknowledge and celebrate your progress, whether it's mastering a new feature or completing a course.

7.2 Find Accountability Partners

Partner with a colleague or friend to share learning goals and progress, keeping each other motivated.

7.3 Reflect on Your Growth

Regularly review how your new skills have improved your efficiency, project outcomes, and career prospects.

---

8. Recommended Learning Roadmap

Time Frame	Learning Objective	Resources
Month 1	Explore advanced Microsoft Project features	Microsoft Learn tutorials, LinkedIn Learning courses
Months 2–3	Integrate Power BI for advanced reporting	Power BI and Microsoft Project integration guides, webinars
Months 4–6	Gain familiarity with Agile and hybrid methodologies	Online Agile courses, Scrum certifications
Month 7	Join and engage in professional communities	Microsoft forums, LinkedIn groups, local meetups
Months 8–12	Pursue a professional certification	PMP, Microsoft Certified: Project Manager Associate, or Certified Scrum Master (CSM) exams

9. Conclusion

Planning your ongoing learning path is essential for maintaining expertise and staying relevant in the ever-evolving field of project management. With a structured approach, commitment to continuous improvement, and utilization of available resources, you can master new skills and elevate your project management capabilities.

Key Takeaways:

- Continuous learning ensures you stay updated with the latest tools and methodologies.
- Leverage Microsoft and third-party resources, certifications, and communities to enhance your expertise.
- Practice and apply your knowledge regularly to solidify skills and demonstrate value.

The next and final section will focus on summarizing key takeaways and common pitfalls to avoid as you continue your journey with Microsoft Project.

Section XIV:
Conclusion

Key Takeaways and Best Practices

As you wrap up your journey through *Mastering Microsoft Project: From Setup to Success*, it's essential to distill the core lessons and strategies that can elevate your project management expertise. This chapter highlights the key takeaways from the book and outlines best practices for effectively using Microsoft Project to manage projects from start to finish.

Key Takeaways

1. Microsoft Project is a Versatile Tool

- **Broad Capabilities**: Microsoft Project is a powerful platform for planning, scheduling, resource management, progress tracking, and reporting. It caters to projects of all sizes and industries.
- **Integration**: Seamless integration with Microsoft 365 tools enhances collaboration and productivity.

2. Foundational Steps Lead to Success

- **Setup Matters**: Proper configuration of project calendars, working times, and default settings ensures a strong foundation for accurate scheduling and tracking.
- **Clear Objectives**: Define clear project goals, milestones, and deliverables to guide all phases of project management.

3. Mastering the Planning Phase

- **Task Management**: Breaking down work into manageable tasks, setting dependencies, and defining milestones creates a robust project plan.
- **Resource Allocation**: Thoughtful resource planning and management prevent overallocation and maximize team efficiency.

4. Scheduling and Baselines are Critical

- **Dynamic Scheduling**: Leverage task dependencies, durations, and constraints to create flexible schedules that accommodate real-world changes.
- **Baseline Comparisons**: Setting and regularly reviewing baselines helps measure project performance against initial plans.

5. Tracking Progress Enhances Accountability

- **Regular Updates**: Consistently update tasks, resources, and timelines to maintain an accurate view of project status.
- **Performance Monitoring**: Use built-in tools like timescales, Gantt charts, and custom views to track progress and identify potential risks.

6. Effective Reporting and Communication

- **Customizable Reports**: Utilize built-in and custom reports to communicate project status, progress, and forecasts to stakeholders effectively.

- **Stakeholder Engagement**: Regular communication ensures alignment with goals and fosters trust in the project's progress.

7. Adaptation and Scalability

- **Agile and Hybrid Approaches**: Adapt Microsoft Project to support both traditional and modern project management methodologies.
- **Multi-Project Management**: Leverage features like master projects, subprojects, and resource pools for managing complex, interdependent projects.

8. Continuous Learning and Improvement

- **Stay Updated**: Keep pace with software updates, new features, and emerging project management trends.
- **Lessons Learned**: Regularly capture and analyze lessons from completed projects to improve future processes and outcomes.

Best Practices for Using Microsoft Project

1. Start with a Well-Defined Plan

- Gather all project requirements before opening Microsoft Project.
- Clearly define the scope, objectives, stakeholders, and deliverables.

2. Utilize Templates for Efficiency

- Use pre-built templates to save time and ensure consistency.
- Create custom templates for recurring project types within your organization.

3. Keep Data Organized

- Maintain a clean and logical task hierarchy with clear naming conventions.
- Use custom fields to capture project-specific information efficiently.

4. Leverage Views and Filters

- Switch between different views (e.g., Gantt Chart, Resource Usage, Task Sheet) for deeper insights.
- Use filters and groupings to focus on specific data subsets relevant to your needs.

5. Manage Resources Wisely

- Assign resources carefully, considering availability and workload.
- Regularly check for overallocations and resolve conflicts promptly.

6. Update Regularly and Consistently

- Schedule regular update intervals to keep the project plan accurate.
- Train team members to provide timely and precise updates for tasks assigned to them.

7. Monitor Risks and Adjust

- Use the Critical Path method to identify and manage potential delays.
- Adjust schedules, resources, or priorities proactively to address emerging challenges.

8. Communicate Effectively

- Share project plans and updates with stakeholders using clear visuals and reports.
- Customize communication based on the audience, focusing on their specific concerns.

9. Automate Repetitive Tasks

- Use macros and automation features to reduce manual effort and enhance efficiency.
- Customize formulas to automate calculations and advanced tracking metrics.

10. Reflect and Learn

- Conduct post-project reviews to gather insights from the team and stakeholders.
- Archive project plans and documentation for future reference.

Conclusion

Mastering Microsoft Project is an ongoing journey that involves applying best practices, staying updated with evolving features, and continuously refining your project management skills. By leveraging the insights and techniques outlined in this book, you can:

- Plan and execute projects more effectively.
- Improve collaboration and communication.
- Deliver projects on time, within scope, and on budget.

Whether you're managing a single project or overseeing a portfolio, Microsoft Project is a reliable tool to help you achieve success. Use this knowledge as a foundation to build your expertise and drive impactful results in your projects.

Common Pitfalls and How to Avoid Them

Microsoft Project is a robust and feature-rich tool, but like any software, its effectiveness depends on how it is used. Many project managers encounter common pitfalls that can hinder their success. This chapter focuses on identifying these challenges and providing actionable solutions to avoid or overcome them.

1. Overloading the Project Plan

The Pitfall

- Including too much detail, such as overly granular tasks or excessive custom fields, can make the project plan unwieldy and hard to manage.

How to Avoid It

- **Focus on Key Tasks**: Include tasks that are significant to the project's success. Avoid breaking tasks into unnecessary sub-tasks unless required.
- **Use Filters and Views**: Customize views to display only the essential information for different stakeholders.
- **Maintain Simplicity**: Keep the project plan streamlined while still capturing critical details.

2. Ignoring Baselines

The Pitfall

- Failing to set baselines makes it impossible to measure project performance against the original plan.

How to Avoid It

- **Set Baselines Early**: Establish a baseline as soon as the project plan is approved.
- **Update Baselines Judiciously**: Re-baseline only when significant changes to scope or objectives occur.
- **Monitor Regularly**: Compare baseline data with actual performance to identify deviations and take corrective actions.

3. Poor Resource Management

The Pitfall

- Assigning resources without considering their availability or overall workload can lead to overallocation, resource burnout, and project delays.

How to Avoid It

- **Use Resource Calendars**: Set up resource calendars to reflect availability and working hours.
- **Monitor Workloads**: Regularly check the Resource Usage view for overallocation.
- **Level Resources**: Use Microsoft Project's resource leveling feature to distribute workloads effectively.

4. Neglecting Stakeholder Communication

The Pitfall

- Infrequent or unclear communication with stakeholders can lead to misaligned expectations and dissatisfaction.

How to Avoid It

- **Tailor Reports**: Use Microsoft Project's built-in and custom reporting tools to provide stakeholders with clear, concise updates.
- **Schedule Updates**: Share progress reports at regular intervals or as milestones are achieved.
- **Engage Stakeholders**: Use visual aids like Gantt charts or dashboards to ensure stakeholders understand the project's status.

---

5. Rigid Scheduling

The Pitfall

- Creating a rigid project schedule that cannot accommodate unforeseen changes can result in missed deadlines and unrealistic expectations.

How to Avoid It

- **Use Task Dependencies**: Establish logical links between tasks to create a dynamic schedule.
- **Build Buffers**: Include contingency buffers for high-risk activities.
- **Monitor the Critical Path**: Regularly review and adjust the critical path to keep the project on track.

---

6. Failure to Track Progress Regularly

The Pitfall

- Delaying updates to the project schedule can cause inaccurate reporting and missed issues.

How to Avoid It

- **Regular Updates**: Update task progress, resource usage, and costs frequently.
- **Set Milestones**: Use milestones as checkpoints for measuring progress.
- **Use Custom Views**: Create views that highlight incomplete tasks or those falling behind schedule.

---

7. Misusing Constraints

The Pitfall

- Overusing or misapplying constraints can limit the flexibility of the project schedule.

How to Avoid It

- **Use Constraints Sparingly**: Apply constraints only when absolutely necessary, such as for fixed deadlines.
- **Rely on Dependencies**: Use task dependencies instead of constraints to manage task relationships.
- **Review Constraints**: Regularly check the Task Inspector to identify and resolve conflicts.

8. Lack of Customization

The Pitfall

- Relying solely on default settings and views can limit the usefulness of Microsoft Project.

How to Avoid It

- **Customize Views**: Tailor Gantt charts, tables, and reports to fit project needs.
- **Use Custom Fields**: Add custom fields to track unique metrics.
- **Leverage Templates**: Create and reuse project templates to save time and maintain consistency.

9. Insufficient Training

The Pitfall

- Lack of knowledge about Microsoft Project's features can lead to underutilization or errors in project management.

How to Avoid It

- **Invest in Training**: Ensure all project team members receive adequate training on Microsoft Project.
- **Utilize Resources**: Use online tutorials, forums, and guides to enhance skills.
- **Practice Regularly**: Encourage team members to practice using Microsoft Project on smaller projects or simulations.

10. Inadequate Change Management

The Pitfall

- Failing to account for scope changes, new requirements, or unforeseen challenges can derail the project.

How to Avoid It

- **Document Changes**: Keep a log of all scope changes and their impact on schedule and budget.
- **Reassess Plans**: Update project plans and baselines to reflect approved changes.
- **Communicate Impact**: Share change implications with stakeholders to align expectations.

Conclusion

Avoiding common pitfalls in Microsoft Project requires a proactive approach to planning, tracking, and communication. By recognizing potential challenges and implementing these best practices, project managers can maximize the effectiveness of Microsoft Project and drive successful project outcomes.

Next Steps for Continued Improvement

As you conclude your journey through *Mastering Microsoft Project: From Setup to Success*, it's essential to focus on the path forward. Mastering Microsoft Project is not a one-time achievement; it's an ongoing process of refinement, adaptation, and learning. This chapter will outline practical next steps to ensure your continued improvement as a project manager using Microsoft Project.

1. Reflect on Your Learning

Review Your Progress

- Take time to reflect on what you've learned throughout this book.
- Identify areas where you feel confident and those where further practice is needed.

Evaluate Your Projects

- Review your completed and ongoing projects. Identify what worked well and where challenges arose.
- Use these insights to improve your planning and execution in future projects.

2. Practice Regularly

Apply Your Knowledge

- Use Microsoft Project for various projects to solidify your skills.
- Experiment with advanced features such as macros, custom fields, and reporting tools.

Work on Simulations

- Create mock projects to practice techniques like resource leveling, critical path analysis, and task dependencies without the pressure of a real deadline.

3. Seek Feedback and Collaborate

Engage with Your Team

- Gather feedback from your team about how effectively you've managed projects using Microsoft Project.
- Collaborate with team members to identify improvements in workflow and communication.

Learn from Stakeholders

- Involve stakeholders in project reviews to understand their perspectives on timelines, deliverables, and reporting.

4. Expand Your Knowledge

Dive Deeper into Features

- Explore advanced topics like Earned Value Management (EVM), integration with third-party tools, or agile project management in Microsoft Project.

Stay Informed

- Keep up with updates and new features in Microsoft Project. Regularly check Microsoft's official blog, forums, or release notes.

---

5. Invest in Continuous Training

Enroll in Advanced Courses

- Participate in advanced Microsoft Project or project management courses to further develop your expertise.

Obtain Certifications

- Consider obtaining certifications like:
    - **Microsoft Project Certification**
    - **Project Management Professional (PMP)**
    - **Certified ScrumMaster (CSM)** (for agile methodologies)

---

6. Join Professional Communities

Network with Professionals

- Join project management forums and LinkedIn groups to exchange knowledge and learn from peers.
- Attend industry conferences and webinars to stay updated on best practices and emerging trends.

Participate in Discussions

- Engage in conversations about challenges and solutions in project management, specifically using Microsoft Project.

---

7. Focus on Personal Growth

Embrace Feedback

- Continuously seek feedback from colleagues, clients, and stakeholders.
- Use constructive criticism as an opportunity to improve your skills and processes.

Set Learning Goals

- Establish specific goals for your growth in project management and Microsoft Project proficiency.
- Regularly assess your progress and adjust your goals as needed.

---

8. Leverage Technology

Adopt New Tools

- Explore add-ons, integrations, and complementary tools to enhance your use of Microsoft Project.
- Test features like Microsoft Teams integration, Power BI reporting, and SharePoint collaboration.

Automate Repetitive Tasks

- Use macros and other automation techniques to reduce manual effort and improve efficiency.

---

9. Emphasize Leadership Skills

Communicate Effectively

- Hone your ability to communicate project updates, risks, and milestones clearly to all stakeholders.
- Use visuals like Gantt charts, dashboards, and timelines to aid understanding.

Build Team Morale

- Foster a positive and collaborative team environment. Recognize achievements and address challenges proactively.

---

10. Start Your Next Project with Confidence

Apply Best Practices

- Begin your next project by incorporating the lessons and techniques learned from this book.
- Use templates, baselines, and a robust planning process to set your project up for success.

Monitor and Adapt

- Continuously monitor your project's progress and adapt to changes effectively.
- Embrace flexibility to address unforeseen challenges.

Conclusion

Your journey with Microsoft Project doesn't end here. By consistently applying the strategies and techniques covered in this book, seeking opportunities for growth, and staying curious about emerging tools and methodologies, you will continue to excel as a project manager. Remember, mastery is a continuous process, and every project is a step toward greater expertise.

Stay committed to learning, improving, and adapting—and you'll lead your projects to success time and time again.

Appendices

Appendix A: Glossary of Project Management and MS Project Terms

This glossary provides definitions and explanations for essential project management and Microsoft Project terms. Use it as a quick reference to understand key concepts and terminology while working with Microsoft Project.

A

- **Activity**: A specific piece of work required to complete a project. Also referred to as a task.
- **Agile Methodology**: An iterative approach to project management that focuses on delivering value incrementally and adapting to changes quickly.
- **Allocation**: The process of assigning resources to tasks in a project.
- **Assignment**: The specific resource allocated to a task, including work effort and duration.

B

- **Baseline**: A fixed reference point in a project plan, used to compare actual progress with the original plan.
- **Buffer**: Extra time or resources added to a project schedule to manage uncertainty or risk.
- **Budget**: The total estimated cost required to complete a project.

C

- **Calendar**: A schedule defining working and non-working days and hours for a project, task, or resource.
- **Constraint**: A limitation or restriction applied to a task, such as a start date or finish date.
- **Critical Path**: The sequence of tasks that determines the shortest time in which a project can be completed.

D

- **Deadline**: The latest date by which a task or project must be completed.
- **Dependency**: A logical relationship between two tasks, such as one task needing to finish before another can start.
- **Duration**: The total amount of working time required to complete a task.

E

- **Earned Value Management (EVM)**: A project management technique for measuring project performance by comparing planned and actual progress.
- **Effort**: The amount of work required to complete a task, typically measured in hours or days.
- **Event**: A significant point or milestone in a project timeline.

F

- **Finish-to-Start (FS)**: A dependency type where one task cannot start until another task finishes.
- **Float (Slack)**: The amount of time a task can be delayed without affecting the overall project schedule.

G

- **Gantt Chart**: A visual representation of a project schedule that displays tasks, durations, and dependencies.
- **Goal**: The intended outcome or objective of a project.

L

- **Lag**: A delay between tasks that have a dependency.
- **Lead**: The amount of time by which a successor task can start before its predecessor finishes.

M

- **Milestone**: A significant event or achievement in a project, often used to measure progress.
- **Microsoft Project**: A project management software tool used to plan, schedule, and track projects.

O

- **Overallocation**: A condition where a resource is assigned more work than can be completed within the available time.

P

- **Percent Complete**: A measure of progress for a task or project, expressed as a percentage.
- **Predecessor**: A task that must be completed before another task can begin.
- **Project Scope**: The boundaries and deliverables of a project.

R

- **Resource**: Any person, equipment, or material required to complete a task or project.
- **Risk**: A potential event or condition that could negatively impact a project's objectives.

S

- **Schedule**: A detailed timeline outlining when tasks and milestones will be completed.
- **Slack (Float)**: See **Float**.
- **Stakeholder**: Any individual, group, or organization impacted by or involved in a project.
- **Subproject**: A smaller project that is part of a larger master project.

T

- **Task**: A specific piece of work within a project. Also known as an activity.
- **Timescale**: The calendar timeframe for displaying tasks in a project schedule.

W

- **Work Breakdown Structure (WBS)**: A hierarchical decomposition of a project into smaller, manageable components.
- **Workload**: The amount of work assigned to a resource within a given timeframe.

Dependencies in Microsoft Project

Types of Task Dependencies:

1. **Finish-to-Start (FS)**: Task B starts only after Task A finishes.
2. **Start-to-Start (SS)**: Task B starts only after Task A starts.
3. **Finish-to-Finish (FF)**: Task B finishes only after Task A finishes.
4. **Start-to-Finish (SF)**: Task B finishes only after Task A starts.

Acronyms

- **EVM**: Earned Value Management
- **FS**: Finish-to-Start
- **SS**: Start-to-Start
- **FF**: Finish-to-Finish
- **SF**: Start-to-Finish
- **WBS**: Work Breakdown Structure

This glossary equips you with a foundational understanding of key terms and concepts in project management and Microsoft Project, enhancing your ability to navigate and utilize the software effectively.

Appendix B: Quick Reference Guide to Common Shortcuts and Commands

This appendix provides a handy reference for common shortcuts and commands used in Microsoft Project. These shortcuts will help you navigate the software efficiently and complete tasks with greater ease.

Keyboard Shortcuts

General Navigation

- **Ctrl + N**: Create a new project.
- **Ctrl + O**: Open an existing project.
- **Ctrl + S**: Save the current project.
- **F12**: Save the project as a new file.
- **Ctrl + F4**: Close the current project.
- **Alt + F4**: Exit Microsoft Project.
- **Ctrl + P**: Print the project.

Task Management

- **Insert**: Add a new task.
- **Ctrl + X**: Cut a selected task.
- **Ctrl + C**: Copy a selected task.
- **Ctrl + V**: Paste a task.
- **Delete**: Delete a selected task.
- **Alt + Shift + Left Arrow**: Indent a task.
- **Alt + Shift + Right Arrow**: Outdent a task.
- **Ctrl + Shift + F5**: Highlight tasks on the critical path.

Navigation within Views

- **F6**: Move between panes in a split view.
- **Shift + F6**: Move to the previous pane.
- **Ctrl + Tab**: Switch between open project windows.

Scheduling and Planning

- **F5**: Go to a specific date in the Gantt Chart.
- **Alt + F10**: Open the Task Information dialog box.
- **Ctrl + G**: Open the Go To dialog box (e.g., specific tasks or dates).
- **Shift + F2**: Open the Task Details dialog box.
- **Ctrl + D**: Open the Task Notes dialog box.

Working with Resources

- **Alt + F10**: Open the Resource Information dialog box.
- **Alt + Shift + F9**: Level resources automatically.
- **Alt + Shift + D**: Open the Assign Resources dialog box.

Views and Tables

- **Ctrl + Alt + F1**: Switch to the Gantt Chart view.
- **Ctrl + Alt + F3**: Switch to the Task Usage view.
- **Ctrl + Alt + F4**: Switch to the Resource Sheet view.
- **F8**: Activate Split View.

Formatting and Customization

- **Ctrl + B**: Bold the selected text or task name.
- **Ctrl + I**: Italicize the selected text.
- **Ctrl + U**: Underline the selected text.
- **Ctrl + Shift + +**: Zoom in.
- **Ctrl + Shift + -**: Zoom out.

Tracking Progress

- **Ctrl + Shift + F12**: Update project progress.
- **Ctrl + F2**: Mark a task as complete.

Common Commands and Ribbon Navigation

Task Tab

- **Add Task**: Quickly create a new task.
- **Link Tasks**: Create dependencies between tasks.
- **Mark as Milestone**: Set a task as a milestone.

Resource Tab

- **Assign Resources**: Allocate resources to tasks.
- **Level Resources**: Balance resource allocation across tasks.

Report Tab

- **Visual Reports**: Generate graphical reports.
- **Custom Reports**: Design and save reports tailored to project needs.

Format Tab

- **Bar Styles**: Adjust styles of Gantt chart bars.
- **Text Styles**: Customize text appearance across views.

Tips for Maximizing Efficiency

1. **Memorize Frequently Used Shortcuts**: Start with shortcuts you use daily, such as saving files or creating tasks.
2. **Utilize the Ribbon Navigation**: The tabs on the ribbon are logically categorized to help you find commands quickly.
3. **Customize Quick Access Toolbar**: Add commonly used commands for even faster access.

This quick reference guide will improve your proficiency with Microsoft Project, enabling you to work smarter and faster while managing your projects effectively.

Appendix C: Recommended Resources for Further Learning

To enhance your mastery of Microsoft Project and project management methodologies, this appendix lists valuable resources for continuous learning. These resources include books, online courses, communities, and tools that can help deepen your understanding and refine your skills.

Books

- **"Microsoft Project Step by Step" by Carl Chatfield and Timothy Johnson**
  A beginner-friendly guide offering step-by-step instructions to navigate Microsoft Project. Perfect for those new to the software.
- **"PMP Exam Prep" by Rita Mulcahy**
  A comprehensive guide to project management concepts and practices, aligned with the PMBOK® Guide. Excellent for aspiring certified project managers.
- **"Agile Practice Guide" by Project Management Institute**
  A great resource for understanding Agile methodologies and integrating them into your project management processes.
- **"Critical Chain" by Eliyahu M. Goldratt**
  A book that provides insights into managing projects with limited resources and tight deadlines using the Theory of Constraints.

Online Courses

- **Microsoft Learn: Microsoft Project Training**
  The official Microsoft platform offers free, self-paced courses tailored to Microsoft Project users of all levels.
  Website: [https://learn.microsoft.com/] (https://learn.microsoft.com/)
- **LinkedIn Learning**
  Courses like "Mastering Microsoft Project" by Bonnie Biafore provide a structured learning path with practical examples.
  Website: [https://www.linkedin.com/learning/] (https://www.linkedin.com/learning/)
- **Coursera**
  Explore project management courses from top universities and organizations, including Microsoft Project tutorials.
  Website: [https://www.coursera.org/] (https://www.coursera.org/)
- **Udemy**
  A platform with various Microsoft Project courses focusing on both foundational and advanced skills.
  Website: [https://www.udemy.com/] (https://www.udemy.com/)

Websites and Blogs

- **ProjectManagement.com**
  A hub for project management articles, tools, and templates.
  Website: [https://www.projectmanagement.com/] (https://www.projectmanagement.com/)

- **MPUG (Microsoft Project User Group)**
  Offers webinars, articles, and certifications specifically tailored to Microsoft Project users.
  Website: [https://www.mpug.com/] (https://www.mpug.com/)
- **Smartsheet Blog**
  Covers project management best practices, tools, and tips.
  Website: [https://www.smartsheet.com/blog] (https://www.smartsheet.com/blog)

Communities and Forums

- **Reddit: r/projectmanagement**
  A community-driven forum to discuss project management challenges, tips, and tools.
  Website: [https://www.reddit.com/r/projectmanagement/]
  (https://www.reddit.com/r/projectmanagement/)
- **Microsoft Community**
  The official Microsoft forum where users can ask questions and share insights about Microsoft Project.
  Website: [https://answers.microsoft.com/] (https://answers.microsoft.com/)
- **LinkedIn Groups**
  Groups such as "Microsoft Project Users" and "Project Management Professionals" offer networking and learning opportunities.

Certification and Professional Development

- **Project Management Institute (PMI)**
  Offers certifications like PMP® and CAPM®, which provide an in-depth understanding of project management practices.
  Website: [https://www.pmi.org/] (https://www.pmi.org/)
- **Scrum Alliance**
  Provides certifications like Certified Scrum Master (CSM®) for professionals interested in Agile methodologies.
  Website: [https://www.scrumalliance.org/] (https://www.scrumalliance.org/)
- **Microsoft Certification**
  Become a certified Microsoft Project expert to validate your skills and enhance your resume.
  Website: [https://www.microsoft.com/en-us/learning/] (https://www.microsoft.com/en-us/learning/)

Additional Tools

- **Templates from Microsoft Office**
  Access a library of free templates for various project types.
  Website: [https://templates.office.com/] (https://templates.office.com/)
- **Gantt Chart Generators**
  Tools like TeamGantt and Smartsheet complement Microsoft Project for visualizing timelines and managing team collaboration.

By leveraging these resources, you can continuously grow your expertise in Microsoft Project and project management, staying ahead in your professional journey.

www.ingramcontent.com/pod-product-compliance
Lightning Source LLC
Chambersburg PA
CBHW080553060326
40689CB00021B/4845